Praise for *The Whole Okra*

"The volume you hold in your hands is a love song long overdue. It is anything and everything you wanted to know about this hallmark ingredient. . . . I leave you in the capable hands of Chris Smith, your leader on a journey through the world of *The Whole Okra*."

—MICHAEL W. TWITTY, author of the James Beard Award–winning book *The Cooking Gene*

"Okra is a contentious vegetable—folks love it or hate it. No one is ambivalent. Well, I am an okra lover, an okra apostle, an okra evangelist —and Chris Smith is my absolute hero. He has written *the* definitive book on okra. *The Whole Okra* is packed with tips, techniques, gardening advice, and recipes. It's an absolute must-have for okra devotees."

—VIRGINIA WILLIS, James Beard Award–winning cookbook author and chef

"Chris Smith takes a deep, deep dive into American okra culture, and the result is this amazing encyclopedia of our most misunderstood vegetable. *The Whole Okra* is a long-anticipated contribution to the foodways of the American South."

—SEAN BROCK, James Beard Award–winning chef and author

"Much maligned, okra is among the most underrated vegetables. Okra is delicious, versatile, plentiful, and worthy of the attention it gets in *The Whole Okra*. If you are an okra lover, this book is an affirmation, filled with interesting stories and great ideas for using pods, flowers, and more. If you are not yet an okra lover, Chris Smith's enthusiasm may well convert you."

—SANDOR ELLIX KATZ, author of *Wild Fermentation* and the James Beard Award-Winning book *The Art of Fermentation*

"Okra has found its champion in Chris Smith as he covers every imaginable use for okra flowers, pods, and stems. Even longtime okra advocates will find plenty of new information here, from growing okra seedlings as microgreens to fermenting perfect pods. With humor and unflagging optimism for his subject, Smith melds meticulous research with firsthand experience working with dozens of varieties of okra. *The Whole Okra* is a celebration for okra fans, and may lead to the conversion of at least a few okra haters."

—BARBARA PLEASANT, award-winning author of *Homegrown Pantry*

"Gardeners and chefs are always looking for resources to inspire creative expression, especially when it comes to bumper crops. Chris Smith has put together a witty and well-written book about okra with historical context and creative uses for one of the South's favorite and most debated exports. Even okra haters will find a recipe or concept in *The Whole Okra* that will bring them into the fold."

—IAN BODEN, founding chef and owner, The Shack

"Chris Smith's *The Whole Okra* is a delight for this confirmed okra lover. The beautiful photos and tempting okra recipes by renowned southern chefs call out to adventurous cooks and gardeners everywhere to try this underappreciated superfood. In this era of climate change, it is exciting to learn about okra's many unique uses as high-protein flour, strong fiber, handcrafted paper, and high-quality oil."

—IRA WALLACE, gardening expert, author of *The Timber Press Guide to Vegetable Gardening in the Southeast*

"Okra has been discovered among the offerings in ancient Greek tombs, uncontestable evidence that this fascinating and well-travelled food plant has a rich history yet to be fully written. Meanwhile there is no need to wait for archaeology to piece it all together. In *The Whole Okra*, Chris Smith has given us an excellent introduction to all you need to know about okra, from hands-on garden tips to the many unusual ways to cook it—not to mention one of the best guides available to the multitude of varieties to choose from."

—WILLIAM WOYS WEAVER,
food historian; author of
Heirloom Vegetable Gardening

"*The Whole Okra* honors the humble yet versatile virtues of okra, and Chris Smith's comical, creative style of writing drew me in from the very beginning. His descriptions of okra's infinite potential will inspire readers to dive deep into the heart and soul of what is possible in the garden and in the kitchen. The simple okra plant guides us into realms of diversity and connectivity and perhaps even offers us a glimpse into the meaning of life."

—KATRINA BLAIR, author of
The Wild Wisdom of Weeds.

"Reader friendly, comprehensive, and massively informed, Chris Smith's *The Whole Okra* champions this versatile green vegetable in the face of those who revile its spines and slime. Part survey of varieties, part multicultural cookbook of historic okra preparations, Smith's narrative is a personal tour of this global plant. He explains why we should cherish open-pollinated heirloom varieties, why we should look beyond the pods to the flowers, seeds, and leaves for culinary gratification, and why we should grow okra if time and property permit. This is the first book to consult if you want to know about okra, its history, its cultivation, and its culinary applications."

—DAVID S. SHIELDS,
Carolina Distinguished Professor,
University of South Carolina

"OMG. Who'd a thought *brilliant* and *marvelous* would be used to describe a book about this most unlikely topic? No garden/foodie geek will be able to put down this insightful, witty, humorous masterpiece."

—FELDER RUSHING,
host of NPR's *The Gestalt Gardener*;
author of *Slow Gardening*

"I was skeptical—a whole book on *okra*? Turns out many others are skeptical, too, and Chris Smith wants to set the record straight, which he does in an entertaining and informative way. You can grow okra as easily as tomatoes, pests are few, and it has good vigor. Eat the pods, seeds, and leaves; okra tastes terrific in a raw salad, too. This unexpected combination of a Brit living in Carolina and writing about okra is a great read. *The Whole Okra* will make you want to start growing and eating okra today."

—CHARLES DOWDING,
no dig gardening expert; creator of
the Charles Dowding No Dig website

THE WHOLE
OKRA

A Seed to Stem Celebration

CHRIS SMITH

foreword by MICHAEL W. TWITTY

CHELSEA GREEN PUBLISHING
White River Junction, Vermont
London, UK

Spicy Okra recipe by Marcus Samuelsson is from *The Soul of a New Cuisine: A Discovery of the Foods and Flavors of Africa*. Copyright © 2006 by Marcus Samuelsson. Used by permission of Houghton Mifflin Harcourt.

Round Steak and Okra Gumbo recipe by Virginia Willis is from *Okra: A Savor the South Cookbook* by Virginia Willis. Copyright © 2014 by Virginia Willis. Used by permission of the University of North Carolina Press. www.uncpress.org

Pickled Okra recipe by Sean Brock is excerpted from *Heritage* copyright © 2014 by Sean Brock. Used by permission of Artisan, a division of Workman Publishing Co., Inc., New York. All Rights Reserved

Okra Fries recipe by Vivian Howard is from *Deep Run Roots* by Vivian Howard. Copyright © 2016 by Vivian Howard. Used by permission of Little, Brown, and Company, an imprint of Hachette Books Group.

Project Manager: Alexander Bullett
Editor: Fern Marshall Bradley
Copy Editor: Laura Jorstad
Proofreader: Caitlin O'Brien
Indexer: Margaret Holloway
Designer: Melissa Jacobson

Printed in the United States of America.
First printing May 2019.
10 9 8 7 6 5 4 3 2 1   19 20 21 22

Our Commitment to Green Publishing

Chelsea Green sees publishing as a tool for cultural change and ecological stewardship. We strive to align our book manufacturing practices with our editorial mission and to reduce the impact of our business enterprise in the environment. We print our books and catalogs on chlorine-free recycled paper, using vegetable-based inks whenever possible. This book may cost slightly more because it was printed on paper from responsibly managed forests, and we hope you'll agree that it's worth it. *The Whole Okra* was printed on paper supplied by Versa Press that is certified by the Forest Stewardship Council.

Library of Congress Cataloging-in-Publication Data

Names: Smith, Chris, 1982– author.

Title: The whole okra : a seed to stem celebration / by Chris Smith ; foreword by Michael W. Twitty.

Description: White River Junction, Vermont : Chelsea Green Publishing, [2019]
  | Includes bibliographical references and index.

Identifiers: LCCN 2019005954| ISBN 9781603588072 (pbk. : alk. paper) | ISBN 9781603588089 (ebook : alk. paper)

Subjects: LCSH: Cooking (Okra) | Cooking, American—Southern style. | Okra.

Classification: LCC TX803.O37 .S65 2019 | DDC 641.6/5648—dc23

LC record available at https://lccn.loc.gov/2019005954

Chelsea Green Publishing
85 North Main Street, Suite 120
White River Junction, VT 05001
(802) 295-6300
www.chelseagreen.com

To my incredible and creative wife, Belle,
and my two little okra pods, Emily and Zoe.
As I was finishing writing this book,
Belle told me, "I think I'm addicted to okra."
It was going to be that or divorce;
it could've gone either way.

CONTENTS

FOREWORD

Dearly beloved, we are here today to sing the praises of or bemoan the ubiquity of our friend and/or foe, *Abelmoschus esculentus, Abelmoschus caillei, Abelmoschus . . .* Let's just say it's better known as *okra*. Okra is slimy, spiny, sticky, and, no matter what color it takes on, always relents in the heat of the cooking pot to a sad, military green. But okra is also the most gorgeous of mallows, with a flower that reminds you of the umbrella of a crinoline-laden belle on a summer afternoon. Okra is filling, fights "the sugar," and dances so well with tomatoes, onions, and corn that nobody remembers a time when the four did not carouse the kitchens of the Afro Atlantic world in search of lusty steam and the heat of a hot chili pepper looking to dance, too.

Okra is a globetrotter. A Svengali. A spy with no shame always wearing the disguise of its last appearance. Okra is Indian to the Chinese. Okra are feminine fingers of a Middle Eastern dowager to the Indians, and an Ethiopian treat to the Arabs before them. Yet okra calls Africa birthplace and home, and fried, boiled, stewed, or roasted it wears aliases that speak to its origin from *gumbo* to *quiavo, fevi,* and *okro.* Even now okra keeps telling stories from its adoption dream time, leading us into new foodscapes.

In the landscapes of plantation slavery in the New World, okra has crossed the color line. Okra becomes food for Creoles—those born in the islands in the shadow of the big house or on the strange crescent of settlement known as Brazil. And yet it is a vegetable—or maybe a fruit—with crossover power to define an American regional culture and its boundaries.

The volume you hold in your hands is a love song long overdue. It is anything and everything you wanted to know about this hallmark ingredient from its nutritional values to its health benefits to dates and timelines to recipes to genetic pedigrees. Dearly beloved, I leave you in the capable hands of Chris Smith, your leader on a journey through the world of *The Whole Okra.*

—MICHAEL W. TWITTY,
author of the James Beard Foundation award-winning *The Cooking Gene*
March, 2019

Emerald. *Photograph courtesy of Peter Taylor.*

In Defense of Okra

In short, okra represents true nobility. The next time you hear people say it is herbaceous, hairy and spineless. I urge you to punch them right in the nose.

—DICK WEST, "In Defense of Okra," 1964[1]

In 2006, at the tender age of 26 (not yet woody), I experienced okra for the first time. I was at a roadside greasy spoon somewhere east of Clayton, Georgia. It was my first time in the United States, visiting an old friend, Snowy, from Wales. Snowy had been living and working in Greenville, South Carolina, for about five years. Practically a local. He pushed a bowl of fried okra toward me.

"It's a southern delicacy," he said. Smiling.

Snowy was having a joke. The grease from the okra saturated the greaseproof paper. The little round lumps looked like sections of wooden dowel, rolled in sawdust and deep-fried. The way Snowy was stifling a laugh; the way he wouldn't take the first bite . . .

Okra was not being taken seriously.

It was slimy, greasy, and tasteless, and only good for playing tricks on tourists. I didn't understand the slime at all. Undercooked egg whites, perhaps. Slug slime or the saliva from the mouth of an alien. The grease I knew well from back home. This was grease that had been used over and over. This was fast-food grease, cheap and nasty. And the taste? I remember none.

That was my first experience with okra, and I understand why some people never give it a second chance. Some people never give it a first one, such is its reputation. I can't tell you how many people responded to the knowledge that I was writing a book on okra with, "Yuck! Okra," or "Ewww, slimy." In an episode of *Good Eats* dubbed "Okraphobia," celebrity chef Alton

Brown said, "If you don't find a way to push past this slime business, you're going to regret it." You are going to regret it! Not embracing okra because it's slimy is like not visiting the Alps because you're scared of heights. You're missing out on so much because of one small, manageable aversion.

In 2012, six years after my first encounter, I experienced okra for the second time. I was back in the US, this time engaged to Belle Crawford. Yes, it is true. I married someone from South Carolina called Belle, which technically makes okra the second southern thing I fell in love with. Belle's family is from a long line of southerners, but they are inclined to break with southern social conventions from time to time. That's how I found myself invited (obligated) to Belle's bridal shower, helping her take part in the awkward ritual of receiving and opening presents in front of a crowd of women I didn't really know.

One present bestowed on us that day changed my life. The gifter was Linda Lee, an old school friend of Belle's who worked as a botanist in Georgia. The gift was a shoebox full of Indian-inspired spices. Being from England, where the national dish is chicken tikka masala, and having traveled to India, I found the spices exciting enough. But hidden within that shoebox was an enigma: a single, dried okra pod.

India is the leading producer of okra, where it is called *bhindi* and eaten widely. So there is a chance I may have eaten okra, hidden in the depths of a curry, sometime in my past and unknowingly. But it was at the wedding shower that I really acknowledged the existence of okra for the first time. Linda explained that the pod, which was filled with okra seed, had come from seed she had bought and grown from a roadside farm stand in Rosman, North Carolina. The okra had been grown by the farmer's family, and saved by the farmer's family, and I now owned a piece of that heritage. This little pod weighed heavy with responsibility and possibility—it was a new feeling. This was before I started working for Sow True Seed, a small seed company in Asheville. Before I had a garden to call my own. Those okra seeds had a history and, if I chose, a future. This was nothing like the throwaway ooze from Clayton, Georgia. This was serious. I was compelled to grow it, and so I did.

I now remember my wedding anniversary by how many years I've been growing that okra (six years); I decided to call it Rosman Wedding. That single pod inspired me to dive deep into the world of okra, perhaps deeper than any British person has ever gone. I admit I am an unlikely champion of okra. Garden writer and humorist Felder Rushing has begun calling me the Okra King of America—it's a funny joke, but I don't lay claim to that title. Nor do I take the enormity of okra's history, or its presence in America, lightly. In West Africa, where okra is widely grown, where people were stolen and enslaved, the Akan people have a concept of a three-part destiny:

okra, mogya, and *sunsum.* One's *okra* is somewhat similar to one's soul, and among the Akan it is believed that a person's *okra* receives their destiny at birth, along with certain attributes to aid in that destiny.[2]

It seems that my *okra* was destined to write a book on okra, and that all the events of my life have led me to this point. As a white British guy, I am fully aware that okra is not a part of my culture or heritage. I have, however, fallen in love with okra and have tried to approach this book with integrity, and a deep appreciation of people and food. While okra is grown and enjoyed around the globe, my experiences with it are in the American South, and so I must always remember and honor all the terrible things that happened to allow okra's presence and my eventual connection with it. I must remember and honor the incredible influence of African Americans on our food culture, and okra is just a small part of it. I am not King Okra, I am okra's humble servant, and as the stars align I find myself stumbling upon discovery after discovery, story after story, variety after variety, use after use, of this completely amazing crop called okra, gumbo, bhindi, lady's fingers, and ochro. But still, I sometimes wonder why am I so excited about okra when the average response is closer to Stephen King's, "Nooo, I don't want okra. No okra. No."[3]

I know there are a lot of other okra fans, fanatics even, out there. And for many okra is ingrained as part of their history and culture. The first time I gave a presentation titled "In Defense of Okra," the random outbursts of okra enthusiasm from the audience surprised, distracted, and delighted me. This book is for all those fans, to vindicate your joy in okra and inspire you to take it to the

From top to bottom: Jing Orange, Gold Coast, Stubby. *Photographs courtesy of Peter Taylor.*

3

This is me in my okra field at Franny's Farm, where I grew more than 60 varieties of okra in 2018. *Photograph courtesy of Belle Crawford.*

next level. But this book is also for okra doubters and haters; in many ways this book is written in defense of okra. Chef Virginia Willis tells us, "Folks love okra or they hate it. No one—veritably no one—is in the middle."

◉ ◉ ◉

This book is an exploration of the whole okra, and by that I mean the whole okra plant and all its varied uses. The slime (chapter 3), the pods (chapters 4 and 5), the flowers (chapter 6), the leaves (chapter 7), and the seeds (chapter 8) all have culinary and medicinal uses. The stalk and fibers of okra are useful, too (chapter 9). Well-known chefs and cookbook authors have shared incredible recipes. Award-winning photographer Peter Taylor has contributed stunning photography. And I've shared many of my DIY-style okra projects (okravations!), including Making Your Own Okra Cosmetics (chapter 3), Making Your Own Okra Seed Flour (chapter 8), and Making Your Own Okra Fiber Paper (chapter 9). And I definitely encourage you to grow your own okra (chapter 10). A friend of mine who read an early version of this manuscript reminded me that I was deep down the rabbit hole of okra. Well, that may well be true, so consider this book an *Alice's Adventures in Wonderland*–style okra adventure.

Introduction

In the bigger picture I'm supporting diversity, open-minded gastronomy, and a seed-to-stem approach to eating and gardening. I have deep concerns about our climate and how our food decisions play a role in contributing to (and potentially mitigating) climate change. I am sure okra can help with food security and the challenges we are to face—most likely in my lifetime, and certainly in my daughters'. Okra has a tenacious ability to produce in all conditions, which will be a critical asset given our headlong dive into melting the Arctic, shifting the jet stream, and the consequential erratic and apocalyptic weather events. I fully believe okra is a crop for resilient agriculture.

I often tell people I'm not an okra expert. Rather, I'm an expert okra enthusiast. The information I'll share in this book may surprise you, but it wasn't a secret. My experiments did not require degrees in science; I am not an okra savant. I think I came to write this book *because* I had no experience of okra. Like a child, I have enjoyed okra with wide-eyed innocence.

"I'm getting a little okra-overloaded," Belle told me partway through the writing of this book. But I love her anyway. I'm also training our three-year-old to appreciate raw okra straight from the stalk. I thought it would be a challenge, but she loves it; the word *slimy* is not in her vocabulary. My eight-month-old, Zoe, munched on some okra seeds the other day. It is a common joke among Turkish farmers that if you are not happy in your family life then you should grow some okra, because you'll get to spend a lot of time away from your wife. Luckily my family joined in with my okra adventure!

The star on top of my last Christmas tree was an open okra pod splayed so that the sides of the pod resembled the points of a star. It was attached to the tree with a cord made from fibers from an okra stalk. The Christmas tree lights strung around the tree had okra pod sheaths attached to them that glowed wonderful reds, greens, and blues. This wasn't just a gimmick; I think okra pods are beautiful. I promise you that in this book, you'll find some way to experience okra (all parts of it) that you never imagined.

Choppee. *Photograph courtesy of Peter Taylor.*

CHAPTER 1

Getting to Know Okra

Okra has been like the awkward girl no one but her family thought had any talent. But just look at okra now.
— KIM SEVERSON, *New York Times*[1]

If you don't know it, it's easy to hate it.
— VIVIAN HOWARD, *Deep Run Roots*

A good friend of mine who leads wild food walks is fond of describing the forest as a big party, and he likens wild food identification to meeting new people at that party. Now, if I were at a party, I would never walk up to someone and say, "Hi, my name's Chris, how best can I use you?" I'd want to get to know the person, I'd ask some interesting questions, and we'd have a conversation. The same is true of plants, and okra is one plant I've met (in the garden, not the woods) that I really liked. I grew up in a world void of okra (Southport, England), but I found myself inexplicably wanting to meet it again and again. I had so many questions.

As a self-educated botanist, I love the history and the taxonomy and the botany of food crops; I am concerned about climate issues and our continuing ability to feed ourselves healthy and nutritious food. I'm a homesteader and a seed saver and I love stories. All of my interests have informed the conversations I've had with okra, and the more I've come to know okra, the more its reputation as a disdained and slimy vegetable that is deep-fried into palatability seems unjust. And yet it's perpetuated over and over.

Celebrity chef Tom Colicchio has remarked, "I hate okra and grated mountain yam for the same reason. They are both slimy."[2] Tom Colicchio is a New York chef, and opinions about okra, like debutantes and evangelical Bible thumping, exhibit a strong north-south divide. It was garden writer

I am an okra fan primarily because of its many edible uses, but okra plants are stunning and can be grown for their landscaping aesthetics alone, especially the red-stemmed varieties.

Barbara Wilde who said okra is the vegetable version of the Mason-Dixon Line.[3] Julia Reed, a southern food writer and self-proclaimed okra lover, wrote, "So few people eat okra (more radishes are grown in this country) that it never even makes it onto the lists of top 10 most hated foods."[4] This feels like a low blow, and also untrue. Okra makes it onto plenty of most-reviled foods lists. I was deeply saddened to learn that Robin Williams was not a fan. He is often quoted as saying, "Okra is the closest thing to nylon I've ever tasted. It's like they bred cotton with a green bean. Okra tastes like snot. The more you cook it, the more it turns into string."

So before we leap into how to use okra, let's begin by getting to know okra. Okra is a member of the mallow family, sharing family ties with cotton (*Gossypium hirsutum*), cocoa (*Theobroma cacao*), durian fruit (*Durio zibethinus*), balsa wood (*Ochroma pyramidale*), hibiscus (*Hibiscus* spp.) and the genus *Ceiba* (from which kapok fiber is derived). That would make for a strange family reunion. Durian fruit is surely the family outcast, making okra's dubious reputation seem positively golden. Food writer Richard Sterling has written of durian, "Its odor is best described as . . . turpentine and onions, garnished with a gym sock. It can be smelled from yards away." Durian is a spiny-skinned tree fruit that has earned its very own red-crossed prohibition signs on public transport systems across Southeast Asia. Exotic but malodorous. If Durian showed up at a Mallow Family reunion party, Okra might strut about the room; Okra might not feel so bad about itself. Disdained as it is, I know of no public bans on okra.

But then Cocoa would turn up, fashionably late of course. Rich and famous. World-renowned as the key ingredient in chocolate, more recently rebranded as a superfood, and loved by everyone. There's no competing with that. Okra would retreat to the shadows of the reunion, critically comparing itself with its family members and coming up short, as is the southern way.

If I found myself invited to the Malvaceae family reunion, I would make it a point to sit next to Okra. I've always been drawn to the black sheep of the family. I'd offer the same advice I have given my wife: "Be your lovely self and screw family expectations." I may take it one step further and tell Okra to forget its family and focus on its genus, *Abelmoschus* (pronounced ab-el-MOS-kus), or better yet, its species, *Abelmoschus esculentus* (ess-kew-LEN-tuss).

"Does *esculentus* mean 'worse than radishes'?" I ask.

"No," Okra mumbles, head still hanging. Both of us ignore Cocoa rubbing elbows with Cotton at the pickle table.

"Does *esculentus* mean 'snotty string beans'?"

"No."

"Does *esculentus* mean 'slimy'?"

"No!" A little spark from Okra. My pep talk working.

"How about 'good to eat'?"

"Yeah, I guess," says Okra.

"'Full of food, succulent'?"

"Yes."

"'Delicious and nutritious'?"

"*Yes!* That's me. *Abelmoschus esculentus.* Delicious."

You can't argue with Latin.

The botanical taxonomy is a little jumbled, but basically okra used to be *Hibiscus esculentus* and was later reclassified as *Abelmoschus esculentus.* Today the terms are used interchangeably, despite *A. esculentus* being the accepted taxonomy. The fact that *esculentus* means "full of food" and "delicious" seems to have been forgotten by a large proportion of the North American population. I know all vegetables will have their detractors, but okra seems alone in the way it is disliked. When someone tells you they don't like avocado or eggplant, they do so apologetically, accepting the fault is theirs. But when okra is disliked, it is with negative vehemence for the vegetable itself. That's simply not fair.

Okra lays claim to nutritional and medicinal qualities that remain uncelebrated. It has a panoply of culinary traditions all over the world. Okra is easy to grow and highly productive. But it's the multiple culinary uses of a single crop that really appeal to me. Okra is abounding in food. I'm a permaculturist at heart, and I love it when I find secondary, tertiary, and quaternary yields from the things I grow: Radish seedpods are spicy and yummy, corn silks are

Okra Nomenclature Trivia

In 1753 Linnaeus listed okra as *Hibiscus esculentus* under the subsection *Abelmoschus*. In 1787 Medikus elevated the subsection *Abelmoschus* to its own genus, placing it under the tribe of *Hibiscus*, leaving okra with the species binominal of *Abelmoschus esculentus*. In 1824 De Candolle suggested again that *Abelmoschus* should be a section of *Hibiscus*, which led to all *Abelmoschus* species having *Hibiscus* synonyms. In 1890 Schumann pushed *Abelmoschus* back to genus level, although his reasons were disputed. In 1924 Hochreutiner discovered a defining difference, and the use of *Abelmoschus* as genus was widely accepted.

medicinal, broccoli stems are great peeled and roasted. When it comes to multiple yields from single crops, I put okra on a pedestal and say to all the other vegetables, "Look at the wondrous Okra, you could really learn something." With okra, you can eat the pods, the leaves, the flowers, *and* the seeds. And we're not just talking famine food; we're talking superfood. The plant is packed with vitamins and minerals and phytonutrients.

"*Super* is not the S-word people usually use to describe me," says Okra, still morose.

"You're just misunderstood," I say.

I pull a copy of *Lost Crops of Africa*, volume 2, *Vegetables* out of my bag and read aloud: "'A perfect villager's vegetable, okra (*Abelmoschus esculentus*, Malvaceae) is robust, productive, fast growing, high yielding, and seldom felled by pests and diseases. It adapts to difficult conditions and can thrive where other food plants prove unreliable. Among its useful food products are pods, leaves, and seeds. Among its useful non-food products are mucilage, industrial fiber, and medicinals. Seen in overall perspective, this often-derided resource could be a tool for improving many facets of rural life.'[5]

"See," I say. "Perfect!"

"'Often-derided,'" says Okra.

"It's an American text. That's a reference to American derision. But in reference to your homeland, you are the perfect villager's crop. Perfect!"

"I don't even know where home is," Okra complains.

Sadly it's true. Okra is most likely a cultigen, meaning a plant that was produced by selective breeding. But the original ancestors of okra are somewhat disputed among botanists, with its parents described as "putative" and "possibly."[6] It has all the workings of behind-your-back gossip, which is the last thing you want to be the subject of at a family reunion: Okra, the sad little child of unknown parentage. Oh, how they whisper.

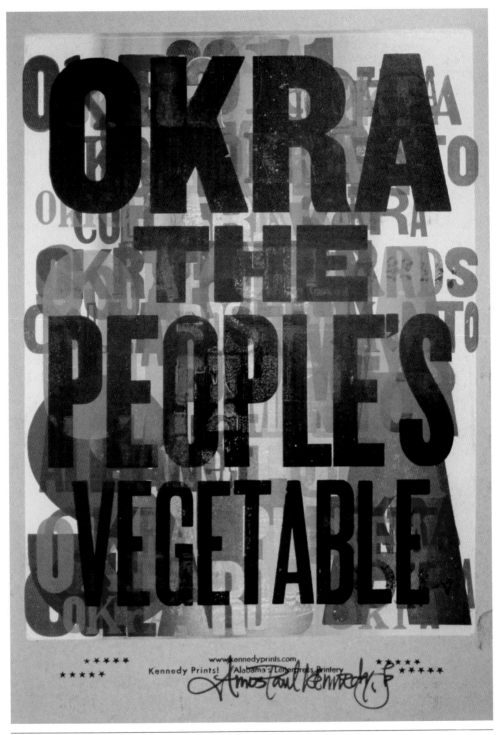

This poster was created for the Burkville, Alabama, Okra Festival by artistic printer Amos Kennedy. According to Kennedy, it was event co-founder Barbara Evans who coined the phrase *Okra, The People's Vegetable*. *Artwork courtesy of Kennedy Prints.*

Okra's closest family connections consist of a small group of species within the genus *Abelmoschus*, which is differentiated from *Hibiscus* mainly by its flower structure—in technical terms it has a calyx attached to the corolla, and the calyx splits and falls off after flowering. The word *Abelmoschus* is from the Arabic *abu-l-mosk* or "father of musk," referring to the scent of the seeds. This characteristic is most clearly seen in *Abelmoschus moschatus*, which is native to India, China, and Southeast Asia and commonly known as musk mallow. *A. moschatus* is commercially grown for its musk-scented seeds, which have long been used in the perfume industry, but it also has edible leaves and pods. The other cultivated species that shares many of the same characteristics is *Abelmoschus manihot*, a native of southern China, India, and Nepal and commonly known as *aibika* or *bele* in Southeast Asia. It produces lush, large leaves that are a popular cooked green in the Pacific Island nations. These three species have similar hibiscus-esque showy flowers and okra-like seedpods, and they grow as erect, herbaceous shrubs.

A handful of wild relatives distributed between Africa and Asia form the basis of the dispute over okra's true origin. The existence of a wild relative, *Abelmoschus ficulneus*, is used to support an East African origin story, although the same species is also found wild in Asia. *A. ficulneus*, aka white wild musk mallow (for its white flower), is well known for its high-quality fiber, and its seeds, stems, and roots are all edible.

Ancient cultivation of okra in East Africa is a strong argument supporting its origin there. *The Encyclopedia Britannica*, 1911, noted, "It [okra] was one of the esculents of Egypt in the time of Abul-Abbas al-Nebati, who journeyed to Alexandria in 1216."[7] Apart from being a great and relevant use of the word *esculent*, this extract introduces the botanist and scientist Abul-Abbas al-Nabati, a Spanish Arab born in Seville. Based on his travels in Africa, he wrote the book *Botanical Journey* and is credited with the earliest written reference to okra. According to the *Pharmacopoeia*, 1879, he "described in unmistakable terms the form of the plant, its seeds and fruit, which last he remarks is eaten when young and tender with meat by the Egyptians."[8]

Nikolai Vavilov, a prominent Russian and Soviet agronomist, botanist, and geneticist, placed okra in the Abyssinian center of origin of cultivated plants, which includes modern-day Ethiopia and the hill country of Eritrea.[9] The presence of "wild" okra reported in the Nile Valley in Nubia, Kordofan, Senaar, Abyssinia, and the Baar-el-Abiad[10] has also been used to argue in East Africa's favor, although many commentators suggest this is a case of a domesticated species gone feral as opposed to a true wild okra.

Today okra is grown across most of the subtropical regions of the earth and is known by many names. But it is the Arabic word for "okra," *bamiyah*, that Abul-Abbas al-Nabati employed. The Ethiopian origin theory suggests that okra traveled from Ethiopia to the Arabian Peninsula via the Red Sea. From there it likely reentered northern Africa via the Sahara as well as continuing its journey east into India and Southeast Asia. The absence of an Indo-Persian word for "okra" is used as evidence that okra traveled from Africa to Asia and not the other way around. In addition, there is no documentation of okra being cultivated in India's pre-Christian Era.

Supporters of the Asian origin theory note that India and Southeast Asia lay claim to a strong center of diversity within the genus *Abelmoschus*. Most of okra's wild relatives exist in the Asiatic region, with *Abelmoschus tuberculatus*, another possible parent, endemic to Uttar Pradesh in northern India. Other wild species include *Abelmoschus angulosus* (found in Southeast Asia), an erect-growing shrub with pale yellow to white flowers. And *Abelmoschus crinitus*, from southern China and Southeast Asia, is a perennial shrub that bears yellow flowers with a purple center.

One conclusion that partially satisfies both sides of the debate is that Asia is the likely "ancestral home" of *A. esculentus*, but okra was domesticated in East Africa.[11] While the exact route and transfer of seeds is lost to antiquity, there is potential to narrow the discussion with genetic analysis of wild and cultivated species. A brief look at the genetics of okra shows a wide diversity, which could support multiple origin stories.[12]

Finally, West Africa is third in line for possible okra origins with the endemic relative *Abelmoschus caillei*, aka West African okra. However, *A. caillei* is a cultigen that originated from a cross between *A. esculentus* and *A. manihot*[13] with culinary uses very similar to okra. *A. caillei* is found only in West Africa and so can more definitely be said to have originated there, but it's a child of okra, not a parent. Both *A. esculentus* and *A. caillei* have been cultivated in West Africa for a long time, with okra showing up in the "archaeobotanical assemblages of savanna sites" as early as the first millennium CE.[14] One West African study noted that 100 percent of the ethnic groups surveyed used *A. caillei* as a food crop; additional uses included "medicine, rope, fuel and mythical."[15] Okra is also widely cultivated in West Africa, and without a doubt West Africa is the origin of the okra that arrived in the Americas during the slave trade.[16]

Okra's arrival in the Americas is more clearly documented. UCLA geography professor Judith Carney outlined the origins and trajectories of each of Africa's major native crops that were brought to the United States on slave ships. "To look at these plants is to engage the organization of the slave trade as corridors for the diffusion of African plants to the Americas," she wrote in *In the Shadow of Slavery*. Many common foods in the US are of African origin, and it is disappointing and disrespectful how little that food

A Select Timeline of Okra's Arrival in the Americas

1648 Dutch naturalist Willem Piso publishes *Historia Naturalis Brasiliae*. This natural history is based on observations of flora and fauna from Piso's trip to Brazil in 1637. He identifies three African food crops: guinea squash, sesame, and okra.

1689 Botanist Paul Hermann composes an herbarium of useful plants found in Suriname. A dried okra leaf resides within—perhaps the oldest in existence.

1707 Natural historian Sir Hans Sloane publishes his *Natural History of Jamaica* based on his time there from 1687 to 1689. He writes that okra flourishes in Jamaica; four pages in his herbarium detail okra plants and pods.

1700s The Reverend John Lindsay, rector of Thomas Ye Vale in Jamaica, produces *The Elegancies of Jamaica*, a collection of watercolors depicting plants, fish, and insects. The volume on plants includes a detailed painting of an okra plant, along with harvested pods.

1748 Peter Kalm, a Finnish Swedish botanist and explorer, is commissioned by the Royal Swedish Academy of Sciences to collect indigenous seeds and plants for agricultural purposes. In *Travels into North America*, later translated by Adolph Benson, Kalm mentions that okra is grown in gardens in Philadelphia and is "reckoned a dainty by some people and especially by the negroes."[17]

1780 Robert Squibb makes the transatlantic journey from England to Charleston, South Carolina, perhaps a century or two after okra but certainly under better circumstances (he wasn't abducted). By 1785 Squibb leases a large plot of ground on Meeting Street near

Rumney Bridge and operates a nursery. Advertisements for his nursery appear regularly in the *South Carolina Gazette*. In 1787 Squibb publishes *The Gardener's Calendar*, which advises sowing okra in March and April.

1781 Thomas Jefferson famously (but as a slave owner, not surprisingly) grows okra. In *Notes on the State of Virginia*, begun in 1781, Jefferson records that the gardens of his native state "yield muskmelons, watermelons, tomatoes, okra, pomegranates, figs, and the esculent plants of Europe." (Again with the esculent!)

1785 Luigi Castiglioni, an Italian botanist, notes in his book *Viaggio* that, in Carolina Low Country, Blacks cultivate a plant "brought by Negroes from the west coast of Africa and is called okra by them."[18]

1792 The English sea captain Hugh Crow, in his published memoirs, notes that at the port of Bonny (in Nigeria) and throughout West Africa, there was no want of "ocra" and that it is "well known throughout the West Indies as an ingredient in making soup."[19]

1804 Bernard McMahon, Thomas Jefferson's garden mentor, is credited with the first extensive seed catalog: *A Catalogue of American Seeds*. The catalog contains the following entry: "Hibiscus esculentus—Eatable hibiscus (or Okra)." Okra is also listed in McMahon's *American Gardener's Calendar* from 1806.

1813 At Monticello, his Virginia plantation, Thomas Jefferson edges his "square" of tomatoes with okra.

1824 Okra recipes begin turning up in cookbooks. *The Virginia Housewife* by Mary Randolph includes a soup and a couple of stews. These recipes are undoubtedly based upon the knowledge of enslaved black cooks (who were not allowed to read or write).

heritage is recognized. PB&J, the great American food, relies on peanuts that originated in Africa. Watermelon, another African food crop, is a favorite for July Fourth picnics and pool parties. Black-eyed peas—cooked ubiquitously for the New Year—are African. And the list goes on.

Jessica Harris, cookbook author and expert on food and the African Diaspora, has said, "Wherever okra points its green tip, Africa has been, and the trail of trade evidenced by the presence of the pod is formidable."[20] It is unclear exactly when okra seeds crossed the Atlantic, but they began showing up in reports in South America in the 1600s, and those reports gradually moved north. Okra almost certainly landed in the US through the ports of Charleston and New Orleans in the 1700s. In *Farming While Black*, Black Kreyol farmer Leah Penniman wrote of her ancestors' reaction to the frequent abductions during the slave trade, "As insurance for an uncertain future, they began the practice of braiding rice, okra, and millet seeds into their hair."[21] I asked Jessica Harris about this, and she expressed some skepticism: "The terror of being abducted, enslaved and forced to endure the Middle Passage makes me think it unlikely that seeds traveled this way." It's hard to imagine what it was like to live on the west coast of Africa at that time, but both seeds and people are miraculous, and Penniman noted that anthropologists have supported stories like those told in her family. However, I think the large-scale adoption of African crops was a form of slave owner control. Consider the sheer numbers of people who were enslaved and the time in which this was happening. America was recently "discovered." Port towns were popping up as pioneer towns. Land was being grabbed and developed. America, like the pyramids, was built on the backs of the enslaved. This was a business—a terrible, horrible, profitable business. And the slave traders knew what they were doing. Award-winning author and culinary historian Michael Twitty explained, "The ample primary sources that read as early ethnographies were really guides to inform contemporary traders about the ups and downs and ins and outs of enslaving and exporting specific ethnic groups and Africans from distinct regions. Understanding the food of the people you were enslaving was critical; it ensured they would be well fed on the perilous Middle Passage and when they arrived in the New World."[22]

Is it a victory for an enslaved people to know their food culture came to dominate southern foodways? That despite the terror and trauma and repression, the food culture influenced many things to come? I think it could be, if the recognition of that history is married with a celebration of the depth and breadth of culinary Africa. Twitty wrote, "For enslaved cooks, okra was a common thread in their mixed African heritage. To the Wolof people it was kanja, to the Mandingo, kanjo, to the Akan it was nkruman and to the Fon, fevi."[23] A common derivative for okra in the Bantu languages is *gombo*, to the Kimbundu *kingombo* and the Lucazi *cingombo*, which forms the use of the word *gumbo* as a synonym for "okra."[24] But okra has influenced food cultures way beyond New Orleans gumbo and the American South.

Okra is ubiquitous across the tropical and subtropical regions of the world and is known by many names: *lady's finger* in English, *bhindi* in Hindi, *tindisha* and *gandhamula* in Sanskrit, *bamia* in Arabic, *huangsukui* in Chinese, *Ts'aukw'ai* in Cantonese, *gombo* in French, *ocker* in German, *quingombo* in Portuguese, *krachiap khieo* in Thai, *bamiya* in Hebrew, *ocra* in Italian, *okura* in Japanese, *bendi* in Malaysian, and *kopi arab* in Indonesian. And along with all these areas of cultivation come distinct uses of okra.

I return my attention to the family reunion and look at Okra sadly sitting next to me, pedunculated stem sagging under the weight of its reputation. This botanical and historical journey does not seem to have inspired Okra. I am confused. All evidence points toward okra's great promise as a food crop. It's as if when vegetables received their marketing representatives for the 20th century, okra got a dud deal.

I nudge Okra with my elbow. "Maybe we should mingle?" I say.

"Nobody likes me," says Okra.

"A teacher once told me that from a distance, all differences are amplified, but up close we see only similarities. This is why we must travel."

"But I'm spiny and I'm slimy," says Okra.

"This is a Malvaceae family reunion. Slime is in your genes. Look over there at *Malva neglecta*, a common weed with neglect in its name, but medicine in its roots and leaves. And there's the *Hibiscus* genus, hanging out together and flaunting their beautiful flowers. *You* have the same flower."

Okra casts a curious look about the room.

"We're going to show them who you really are," I say. "Consider this an exercise in rebranding."

"Who am I?" asks Okra.

"You are Okra," I say. "The perfect villager's crop. The People's Vegetable."

White Velvet. *Photograph courtesy of Peter Taylor.*

CHAPTER 2

Okra, The People's Vegetable

In reality okra could have a future that will make people puzzle over why earlier generations failed to seize the opportunity before their eyes. In the Botanical Kingdom it may actually be a Cinderella, though still living on the hearth of neglect amid the ashes of scorn.

—*Lost Crops of Africa*, volume 2, *Vegetables*

Actually, of course, okra is one of the most heroic of all vegetables. It has done far more for mankind than mankind generally realizes.

—DICK WEST, "The Okra Papers," 1964[1]

The deeper I delve into the world of okra, the more I realize just how many varieties there are. A few years ago I started to catalog and collect the varieties that exist or have existed in the US, with the aim of preserving the genetics and researching the differences. That list is always growing, but at the time of this writing I have gathered more than 150 named varieties and stored them at the climate-controlled seed storage facility in Asheville, North Carolina, belonging to Sow True Seed (the company I work for). In 2018 I grew 76 varieties of okra as part of an observational trial; this year (2019), I will grow another entirely different 76 varieties. That's a lot of okra, but my okra collection is puny compared with that of the USDA Germplasm Resources Information Network (GRIN), which is an online searchable database of genetic plant and seed material held by the USDA. A GRIN search for *Abelmoschus esculentus* yields 1,099 accessions (separate records), most of them unnamed. The collection is exciting because it has okra seed gathered from all over the world, with origin countries including Iran, Iraq, Malaysia, Pakistan, Sudan, and Brazil. Even more impressive than the USDA GRIN okra collection is that of the Indian gene bank. The National Bureau of Plant Genetic Resources in New Delhi claims over 4,000 okra accessions.[2] Other countries, notably in Africa and the Middle East, have their own collections of okra, so there are a *lot* of genetic resources and variability out there.

This will all sound staggering to the casual okra observer, but then again, over the course of the 20th century, North Americans grew extremely disconnected from their food. Supermarket shelves are narrow-minded, farmers have to make a living, and the age of experimentation seems like a distant dream. But in our back gardens and on our homesteads, we have the liberty to adventure and reconnect, and one of the joys of okra is that it is so easy to grow. Consider my average summer garden: There's blight on my tomatoes, Mexican bean beetles are hammering my pole beans (every morning my fingers are yellow and slippery from squishing), squash bugs have overrun the melons (I squish these, too, and they smell of Jolly Ranchers), and striped cucumber beetles won't even let the cucumbers get past Go (I will not be collecting $200, nor will I be collecting any cucumbers). Vine borers have toppled my fall pumpkins and are having a good go at my "resistant" butternuts. The heat has forced every annual green to bolt, downy mildew has browned my basil, and cabbageworms are greedily working their way through collards, kale, and any other brassica crop I was foolish enough to plant. But the okra keeps on growing.

I'm a no-spray gardener. I'll prey on bugs all day long and encourage other predators to join me in garden warfare, but I refuse to bring chemicals to the battlefield. Because I have a newborn and a three-year-old, I oscillate between being an inattentive gardener and a gardener who lets loose Godzilla (aka Emily) into the garden. Emily is well intentioned and likes to water (read: drown a single plant), harvest (read: eat all the cherry tomatoes), and dig for worms to feed the ducks (read: make me dig for worms so she can feed the ducks). I'm also a low-input gardener. Three years ago I started with clay and grass; I'm now slowly building soil fertility by adding manure supplied by my neighbor's horse, wood chips from an arborist friend, and cover crops. The soil is visibly improving, worms are moving in, organic matter is mixing with clay and slowly becoming crumbly and dark. I know the squash and the corn and the brassicas want more; they are hungry plants. Some days I look out on the garden and am surprised that anything is bearing fruit. But the okra keeps on growing.

Okra is chiefly grown in the southern states, and as a frost-sensitive annual it certainly likes the heat. But okra only needs a short growing season, most varieties having an average of around 55 days to harvest. If you can grow tomatoes, then you can grow okra, but the farther north you go the more likely you'll need to start okra as transplants before the last frost. Carol

Can You Grow Okra in Containers?

I'm often asked if you can grow okra in containers. The answer is yes, people do grow okra in containers, and the okra does grow. Dwarf varieties that reach 2 to 3 feet tall (0.6–0.9 m) are assumed to be suitable for container growing. But my experience has been that growing okra in a container doesn't always mean the okra is contained. I once planted a dwarf variety, Little Egypt, in a 5-gallon bucket. The okra grew somewhat slowly, but it was a really dry year. The okra flowered and podded, but yields were low, which is not unexpected for a container-grown plant. At the end of the season, I hypothesized that moving the okra bucket into my hoop house would allow me to eke out an extra week or two of pod production. But when I tried to pick up the bucket, it wouldn't move. Roots had grown through the drainage holes and welded the bucket to the ground underneath. After passing through the small drainage hole, the taproot had fattened and continued to grow strong and deep. My attempt to dig it free resulted in snapping off the taproot about 2 feet below the soil surface. Other roots had found other holes and spread, too, although not quite as dramatically as the main root.

Moral of this story: If you choose to grow okra in containers, I suggest selecting the largest container possible for the best results.

Koury, founder of Sow True Seed, successfully grows okra in Massachusetts with no additional care, and chef Virginia Willis told me that she's begun to see more okra at farmers markets up north over the last decade or so. It's definitely time to stop thinking of okra as something that can only grow in the South. While okra is drought-tolerant (it's unlikely to die even without supplemental water), the pod quality and productivity are affected by water. I'd definitely recommend irrigation if you're growing okra in an area with low summer rainfall. Okra also doesn't like cold temperatures overnight: Once it gets down to around 50°F (10°C) at night, pod growth slows.

I cover the specifics of how to grow okra at the backyard and small-farm scale in chapter 10. For now it's enough to enjoy the knowledge that you can (and should) grow okra, and there are a lot of varieties to explore and culinary uses to test. Admittedly, one deep-fried okra tastes much like the next, but even in the category of fried okra, I enjoy varieties with deep ridges to better capture chunks of cornmeal, and with thick pod walls so the slices hold up well after being plunged into hot oil. Choose straight pods for pickling to maximize jar space, and varieties with locules (chambers in the pods) packed with seeds. Choose large pods for drying, because they will lose a lot of mass in the dehydration process. Grilled okra should be smooth-podded for even cooking; raw okra should simply be delicious.

Many people are shocked to hear that you can eat okra raw, but I'll rarely visit my summer garden without munching on a few pods. It's the best way to get a handle on flavor differences. Red Burgundy is a well-known variety that was developed in South Carolina and won an All-America Selections (AAS) award in 1988. (There have only been seven okra varieties awarded this title since the organization's formation in 1932.) Red Burgundy has thin pod walls (a characteristic of many of the red varieties I've tried) and traces of an arugula-esque nutty spice. In *The Beginner's Guide to Growing Heirloom Vegetables*, veteran gardener Marie Iannotti describes Burgundy okra, which is synonymous with Red Burgundy: "Many plants are beautiful and delicious, but I challenge any to top 'Burgundy' okra. It touts beautiful flowers and flushed foliage, and, unlike most okra varieties, it has no spines. The rich, red pods retain their tender crunch as they elongate. 'Burgundy' has a nutty sweetness that adds unique character to common dishes." Eating the red okra raw is the only way to enjoy the color, which is quickly lost with cooking and pickling. (See page 35 for an early-20th-century recipe for Raw Okra Salad.)

Okra as a Superfood

The health benefits of okra are impressive, too. I spoke with Denise Barratt, a local registered dietitian nutritionist, who told me, "It is time to give this neglected vegetable a little more respect in our diet because of all of the value and benefits that it can provide." As a healthy snack in the garden, an addition to a salad, or something to dip in hummus, okra certainly stands up to nutritional scrutiny. Table 2.1 shows okra's high levels of vitamin K, a nutrient important for blood clotting and bone health. One cup (100 g) of raw okra can supply almost 40 percent of the recommended daily value of vitamin C, a known antioxidant important for tissue health. It also contains a moderate level of vitamin A, important for immune health and eye health. Okra contains four of the eight B vitamins, which all affect our energy metabolism and make okra a great choice during pregnancy.[3] Referring to the slippery nature of the birth canal and the traditional belief that eating okra during labor can prevent breech birth and bring easy labor, Michael Twitty remarked, "Everybody came into the world with okra." As well as vitamins, okra has respectable amounts of the minerals magnesium, calcium, and potassium. The American College of Healthcare Sciences has listed okra as a superfood, noting, "High in vitamins A, K, and C with a nice side dish of the mood-boosting mineral, phosphorus, okra is a lovely addition to any soup or an Asian-fusion salad."[4]

One thing I always wonder about when consulting generic nutritional charts is what variety the nutritionists ran these numbers on. Where was that variety grown and how? Do the numbers reflect the diversity of the crop? The diversity of tomatoes is better recognized than that of okra: Just imagine a large gnarly Cherokee Purple next to a thick-fleshed Amish Paste next to a fuzzy-skinned yellow Garden Peach next to a super-sweet Brown Cherry next to a store-bought hydroponically grown generic hybrid tomato. A single nutritional chart can never be accurate for all that diversity, and the same will be true of okra. Breeding for flavor and nutrition has been neglected as shelf life, shipability, and uniformity became key requirements to support our modern industrial food system. Many heirloom varieties were developed in a time when taste was considered of utmost

Table 2.1. Okra nutrition based on 1 cup (100 g) of raw okra

	Amount	**% of daily value**
Calories	33 cal	—
Total fat	0.2 g	—
Carbohydrate	7.5 g	—
Fiber	3.2 g	12.8
Protein	1.9 g	—
Sugar	1.5 g	—
Calcium	82.0 mg	8.2
Magnesium	57.0 mg	14.3
Potassium	299.0 mg	8.5
Sodium	7.0 mg	—
Vitamin C	23.0 mg	38.3
Thiamin	0.2 mg	13.3
Vitamin B_6	0.2 mg	10.8
Folate	60.0 mcg	15.0
Vitamin A	716.0 IU	14.3
Vitamin K	31.3 mg	39.1

Source: Derived from USDA nutrition database.

importance, and fortunately we are seeing a resurgence in breeding for flavor and nutrition with organizations such as the Culinary Breeding Network and the Organic Seed Alliance on the West Coast and The People's Seed and The Utopian Seed Project (my own fledgling nonprofit) in the Southeast. The new food movement is not just farm-to-table, but breeder-to-belly.

Okra is also a great source of dietary fiber, containing good amounts of both soluble fiber (for regulating blood sugar and cholesterol control) and insoluble fiber (for healthy digestive systems). For this reason okra is recommended for controlling blood sugar in diabetics[5] and for gut and colon health. Its ability to bind toxins and stabilize bowel movements means okra is an incredible gut and colon cleanser.[6] A lectin found in it has been researched for its positive effect on reducing breast cancer cell growth,[7] and the mucilage is also a big plus as gums and pectins like those found in okra are thought to help lower serum cholesterol in the bloodstream.[8]

Okra was a favorite of the Olympic athletes at the Beijing Olympic Games, according to Kantha Shelke, a food scientist at Corvus Blue LLC and spokesperson for the Institute of Food Technologists (IFT). And okra may have some other effects to thank for that. "Because of its physiological effects, it has gained some interesting names including 'green panax' in Japan and 'plant viagra' in the USA," Shelke was quoted as saying in *Time* magazine. "The polysaccharides in okra are thought to open up the arteries in a similar way to Viagra."[9] This knowledge was also noted in an early-19th-century text on the medical properties of plants, which described okra as the "main ingredient in gumbos and calalous, a famous dish, luscious and aphrodisiac."[10]

"Luscious and aphrodisiac," repeats Okra, wistfully.

"My friend Nick just came back from Vietnam, where okra is sold as good for fertility and sex drive," I say.

So for all these reasons (and many more), I highly recommend that you add okra pods to your garden grazing habits. A word of warning, though, before you run out to find your nearest okra patch and start munching on the pods like a hungry goat: Many okra varieties are covered in tiny spines called trichomes (guaranteed to lower the libido!). The spines cook out very quickly, but this doesn't help when you're eating okra raw. I learned this the hard way when I bit into the whitish dwarf variety called Little Egypt. Little Egypt had not earned its spineless badge and my mouth felt abused, like I'd eaten too many salt-and-vinegar-flavored chips. This is one drawback to the raw taste test, because mouthfeel affects our perception of taste. When I bit into the raw pods of one variety from Sudan, it felt as though they were coated with shards of glass. It's hard to appreciate flavor potential when concerned about possible medical bills.

Okra Varieties and Okra Breeding

Okra breeding work has often focused on spineless varieties, and led to development of some that are completely smooth and some that are covered with soft, downy hairs.

"We're going to meet your brothers and sisters," I tell Okra.

"*All* of them?" asks Okra.

"Let's start with a celebrity."

Okra rolls its eyes.

Clemson, South Carolina is about 100 miles (161 km) south of my garden in western North Carolina. It gets hot in North Carolina in the summer, too hot for my cloud-tempered, rain-forged British blood. Belle tells me I'm lucky to be living in the mountains where summer heat can be oppressive, but not terrible. She grew up in Columbia, which her father calls the armpit of South Carolina. Not just hot, but humid as the high seas. Like you might drown walking down Main Street. One hour's drive north of Columbia, a little way off I-26, lies the small town of Lancaster. You'd be forgiven for missing the plaque at the corner of Main and Dunlap Streets that reads: HONORING THOMAS H. DAVIS, SITE WHERE HIS FORTY YEAR SELECTION, (1880), OF OKRA LED TO THE NATIONALLY KNOWN VARIETY OF "CLEMSON SPINELESS OKRA" 1939.

In 1939 the *Aiken Standard* reported on the release of Clemson Spineless. They wrote, "A New Variety of Great Promise."[11] This proved true because today Clemson Spineless has an international reputation and could well be the best-known okra out there. This is certainly the case in the US, where every farmer I spoke to either had grown or knew of Clemson Spineless. In 1980 Clemson University released Clemson Spineless 80, which is an improved variety for earlier production and increased yields. But 100 years earlier, Thomas H. Davis was just beginning to apply an extremely simple botanical skill that few gardeners and farmers practice today: selective seed saving.

The story goes that Thomas H. Davis grew okra in his backyard in Lancaster, South Carolina, and noticed that some plants produced pods with fewer spines. He began saving the seeds from the less spiny plants and continued that practice for 40 years. Thomas H. Davis's okra seed could have remained in his family and become one of the many lost family heirlooms that we'll never experience; Thomas H. Davis could have become bored with the project and stopped saving seed; Thomas H. Davis could have died unexpectedly. But what actually happened is that Dora D. Walker, a conservation specialist with the extension service, got her hands on some of the seeds and sent them to R. A. McGinty, vice director of the Sandhill Experiment Station, a branch of Clemson University located in Columbia, South Carolina.

In 1937 the *Gaffney Ledger* reported, "The samples apparently included a mixture of strains, several of which have now been segregated, including types with tall, medium, and dwarf plants, having pods ranging from almost white to dark green in color."[12] McGinty and his colleagues continued to work on the okra variety, creating a uniform dark-green pod without spines, until its official release in 1939. Clemson Spineless was awarded a silver medal from All-America Selections, the first okra to receive an AAS award.

In the same year an okra variety called White Lightning also became an AAS winner, making 1939 the first and only year to have two winning okra varieties. White Lightning is a sadder story; a story of what can so easily be lost to the whims of agriculture. The variety was introduced by the Georgia-based Hastings Seed Company and is listed in their 1938 seed catalog.

Hastings Seed Company continued to list White Lightning in their seed catalogs into the 1950s, with improved strains cropping up along the way. I contacted All-America Selections for more details on White Lightning and received a short reply explaining, "We had a flood a number of years ago

All Varieties Great and Small

I'm a seed saver (hoarder), and exploring the vast diversity of varieties is important to me. I offer you this tantalizing fly-through of some of the diversity you can expect if you choose to grow your own okra. For further specific varietal information based on my growing experience, refer to this book's appendix, "Okra Diversity Trial."

There are fat and thin pods, long and short pods, and all sorts of variations in between. Okra varieties described as dwarf are generally short plants with full-sized pods, not tall plants with short pods. No self-respecting seed company seems ready to boast that their okra varieties produce dwarf pods, but full-sized pods on a dwarf plant are deemed desirable. Perkins Dwarf Long Pod, for example, is a dwarf plant that bears long pods. There is a certain cognitive dissonance among breeders regarding pod length. The common thought is that bigger is better, and it is assumed that the okra pods will be tender when longer. *Longhorn* and *longpod* are common descriptors (Langston Longhorn and Cherokee Long Pod), with one rather bold variety named Louisiana 16-Inch Long Pod (I've grown this one and blow me down with a feather if the pods didn't mature to precisely 16 inches / 41 cm).

Okra comes in all sorts of shapes, sizes, and colors.

However, any market farmer will tell you that they can't sell long pods because no one trusts that those pods will be tender! I hope some consumer education can combat this, because there are plenty of pods that are delicious when longer. Bradford Family Okra is a great example.

Okras described as *cowhorn* tend to curve and twist as they develop, not unlike a cow's horns. Jefferson is reputed to have enjoyed one such variety, and Monticello currently maintains a Cow Horn okra. Varieties with short, fat pods are described as barrel-shaped or stubby. There's even a variety called Stubby, and it wears its moniker proudly.

As well as shapes and sizes, okra comes in a range of colors: Burgundy, Red River, Louisiana Green Velvet, Emerald, Silver Queen, White Velvet, Jing Orange. Hill Country Red is a stubby green pod with red blushing at the tip; other heirlooms share this trait. White okra was considered supreme in the South in the early 1800s,[13] but my experience in growing white varieties is that the pods are very pale green, not true white.

Many heirloom varieties of okra are named for their link to the South, among them Texas Hill Country, Texas Longhorn, Louisiana Long Pod, Louisiana Short, Alabama Red, Clemson Spineless, Fife Creek Cowhorn, Eagle Pass (Texas), Big Ole' Arkansas, and Beck's Gardenville. Okra varieties are also linked to people (presumably the family or individual names of the seed keepers) such as Harlow's Homestead, Bartley Okra, George Sladersky, Uncle Hershel's, Shows Okra, Mr. Moncrieff Okra, Bradford Family Okra and Mr. Bill's Big Okra. There is even a Hitler Okra! The story goes that a platoon of southern soldiers stationed in Germany in World War II snuck into Adolf Hitler's greenhouse and were excited to find okra growing there. Being from the South they knew exactly what to do and boiled some up, using their metal army helmets as pots. They also saved some seed to bring back to America, where it has been grown and saved ever since. The only part of this story I've been able to verify, however, is that Hitler did have a greenhouse.

and all of our older information was lost." That single statement set off my inner apocalypse. It made me think of the recent flooding of the Global Seed Vault on the Svalbard archipelago, which threatened one million different seed varieties. It made me think of Ron Cook, who is a modern-day version of Thomas H. Davis. When growing Clemson Spineless in the 1990s, Cook noticed that a few of the plants put out more branches than the others and saved seeds from those plants. Over the years he continued to select for branchiness, and his production per plant continued to soar. He started calling this okra Heavy Hitter, and his pods per plant averaged in the hundreds. I reached out to Cook in 2017 to see if he would share some seeds. He sent me pictures of severe flooding that he'd experienced that year (his farm is in Oklahoma). His fields had become a river, two hogs were stuck in a pen, and the fencing eventually washed away. (The pigs swam to safety.) Standing water stayed in his fields for over a week. Only two okra plants survived. Cook wrote, "I'll basically just have to start from scratch in 2018 and hope for the best." It makes me think of Hurricanes Harvey and Maria and the tragic flooding. It makes me think of the wildfires on the West Coast. It makes me think of climate change and the fragility of seed, and by extension our food, and by extension us.

"Time to wake up," says Okra.

"And smell the hibiscus," I say.

Janisse Ray, in her wonderful book *The Seed Underground*, wrote, "When seed varieties vanish from the marketplace, they evaporate not only from collective memory but also from the evolutionary story of the earth. Seeds are more like Bengal tigers than vinyl records, which can simply be remanufactured. Once gone, seeds cannot be resurrected."

I have been searching for White Lightning for a couple of years, asking everyone I meet at seed swaps and food and farming events. Gary Smith, an okra seed collector in Alabama, went so far as to send me a small ziplock bag labeled WHITE LIGHTNING. I asked Smith if it was the real deal.

"The White Lightning was given to me by another herbalist who said it was the real deal," Smith told me. "The real issue you will have is germination."

This small package of seeds is the closest I've come to resurrecting the lost All-America Selections award-winning okra variety White Lightning. Sadly, none of the seeds germinated.

He wasn't joking. I soaked the seeds and they all floated (always a bad sign). I stirred them and one of them sank. I planted them with the utmost care, in perfect conditions, and none of them grew. We may never know what White Lightning was truly like, or why it was considered worthy of an AAS award, but the Hastings Seed Company listing of 1938 does give us a clue to its parentage: White Velvet. White Velvet was introduced by Peter Henderson & Company in 1890, and by 1918 Hastings Seed Company had a catalog listing for Hastings White Velvet as an improved early-producing strain. Twenty years later, in 1938, Hastings Seed released Hastings White Lightning.

White Velvet also suffered near extinction, but now has a place onboard the Slow Food Ark of Taste. The Ark has declared itself to be "a living catalog of delicious and distinctive foods facing extinction. By identifying and championing these foods we keep them in production and on our plates." White Velvet is carried by a good number of seed companies, which is fortunate because in my 2018 okra variety trials, the White Velvet section was completely washed away by flooding! Slow Food USA reported that White Velvet was "regarded as the prime variety of the three velvet okras (Green Velvet, Red Velvet and White Velvet)." Of particular note, "In other varieties, okra's spines make prepping the vegetables troublesome but this [White Velvet] variety's smooth velvet fuzz makes it easy to cook, as well as edible raw."

Okra, Diversity, and Climate Change

The seventh and most recent (2017) All-America Selections award winner is an F1 hybrid called Candle Fire. I grew Candle Fire in 2018, planting as late as the beginning of July but still reaping a good September crop of uniform 3-foot (0.9 m) plants bearing smooth red pods that looked like little torpedoes. The F1 hybrid designation tells us that Candle Fire is the child of two pure okra strains that are intentionally crossed to give the uniform and desirable characteristics the variety has to offer. Hybrids have many benefits, but there are also downsides. The major one is that the supply of these hybrid varieties is reliant on the controlling company, because seeds saved from F1 hybrids will not grow true-to-type when replanted the following year. In other words, seeds saved from F1 hybrids won't necessarily produce plants that have the desirable characteristics of the F1 hybrid itself.

In the case of Candle Fire, Known-You Seed Co. owns the proprietary rights to the variety, and the existence of Candle Fire relies on Known-You Seed's commitment to continue crossing the parents and creating the seed. This lack of control when relying on a hybrid hit home for me when I learned the story of Edward Lenoir, aka The Okra Man, at a conference in Chattanooga, Tennessee.

Lenoir grew up in Michigan where he started to cut okra for his mother at 10 years of age (his mother didn't like getting itchy from the spines!). Sixty-two years later Lenoir grows as much as 1,500 pounds (680 kg) of okra every year in Mississippi and has gained a reputation for having the best okra around. When Lenoir was a teenager, he went to an agricultural show and heard about a new variety of okra that Birdseye (the frozen foods company) used. It was called Annie Oakley, and Lenoir swore this was the best okra he had ever experienced. He religiously bought Annie Oakley seeds from Stokes Seeds even when the price reached $400 a pound. At the conference, Lenoir told me that Stokes Seeds had recently decided to discontinue Annie Oakley,

A Little Genetics Review

Remember Gregor Mendel and his peas? A hybrid is created by cross-breeding two separate homozygous parent lines. Let's say one parent is tall, represented by the alleles TT, and one parent is small, represented by the alleles tt. When TT is crossed with tt, the resulting plants have Tt characteristics. If T (tall) is dominant, then all the F1 plants will be tall (hybrid uniformity). Saving the seeds from the F1 plants and growing them out will give us the average genotype of ($\frac{1}{2}$ T + $\frac{1}{2}$ t), which when crossed would lead to $\frac{1}{4}$ TT + $\frac{1}{2}$ Tt + $\frac{1}{4}$ tt. Since TT is phenotypically the same as Tt, then three quarters of the plants in the second generation will be tall and one quarter will be small.

and so The Okra Man, at 72 years of age, had to cast about for a new variety. He thought he may have found it with Jambalaya, which is another F1 hybrid.

I'm glad that Mr. Lenoir has found a replacement seed that can continue to support him, but his story shows that placing our livelihoods in the hands of hybrid seed companies is inherently risky, and that true food security relies on some level of seed sovereignty—that is, the knowledge and ability to save seeds from year to year. The opposite of hybridized seeds are open-pollinated seeds, which are considered to have stable genetics so that seeds saved will grow true-to-type. My Red Burgundy, for example, will create seeds that I can save and regrow next year.

Creating hybrids is very different from what Thomas H. Davis and R. A. McGinty and Ron Cook did, which was to guide an existing okra variety in a certain direction by selecting for desirable traits. This process can also come from intentionally crossing different varieties to create a mix of genetics and then selecting out the desired traits over multiple generations until they show up reliably. Once those traits are stable, the variety can be described as open-pollinated, and open-pollinated varieties that stand the test of time become our heirlooms, which we treasure for their rich history and/or outstanding characteristics. Selective seed saving and plant breeding is something we can do in our back gardens and small farms,[14] and I can't help but wonder what The Okra Man would have come up with if he'd selectively saved seed for the tastiest okra for 62 years. He would not be reliant on Stokes Seeds or their high-priced seed and would probably have a variety that would blow Annie Oakley out of the water!

Nat Bradford is a farmer growing his family's heirloom okra on his family farm in Irmo, South Carolina. The Bradford Family Okra has been

This okra variety originated in Sudan. Its two-tone green patterning is unusual. All okra pods contain rows of seeds sequestered within locules, but the number of locules varies from variety to variety.

grown and selected for flavor for many generations (since pre-1900), and while it looks like Clemson Spineless, it is a vastly improved variety. Bradford markets to chefs in Columbia and Charleston and commands a high price because of the high quality of his okra. Bradford told me that chef Kristian Niemi said he had never tasted such sweet okra, and chef Sean Brock referred to the pearl-like seeds as "okra caviar." Because this okra is open-pollinated, Bradford is fully independent of the whims of large seed companies. Open-pollinated varieties inherently have much wider genetic variance, and heirlooms were bred to be productive in an age before petro-chemical-based high-input agriculture, which makes them much more adaptable than hybrids.

When we look at our current food systems, it quickly becomes obvious that large-scale agriculture is neither healthy nor sustainable. The David Suzuki Foundation lists eating meat-free, buying local and organic, not wasting food, and growing your own as the key ways to support sustainable food systems to mitigate climate change. I'd take it one step further and suggest that we're going to need resilient crops in the face of erratic weather patterns. The 2014 apocalyptic movie *Interstellar* presents a world wrecked by climate change and failing agriculture. Early in the movie the last crop of okra on earth goes up in flames, leaving only corn to feed the world. In my worryingly frequent post-apocalypse thought experiments, I sometimes wonder if any of us would really care about varietal distinctions if we didn't have the supermarket safety net. Are varieties a privilege of the food-secure and a mechanism of capitalism, where we can add value and ownership to something by giving it a name and a floral description? What does crop resilience really look like?

I ask these questions as a seed saver who loves exploring the plethora of seed varieties and their nuanced distinctions. But I acknowledge that the highest resilience comes from the widest genetic diversity, and that's most likely to be achieved through regionally adapted landraces. Our current food production is based largely on hybrids, which produce really well within a narrow set of conditions. Open-pollinated varieties have greater diversity to support more varied conditions. But landraces take it one step further and openly embrace diversity, offering extreme resilience to changing conditions in a sacrifice of uniformity or varietal purity. Joseph Lofthouse, who lives in Paradise, Utah, specializes in creating landrace crops adapted for his short growing season. He has created an okra landrace: "The first year I planted okra, it was a package of seeds from a seed rack. I suppose that it was Clemson Spineless. It did terrible for me. At the end of the growing season, most of the plants had died." Joseph—continuing what I hope you are beginning to see is a pattern—saved seeds from the plants with the traits he liked. In this case he saved seeds from the single plant that survived long enough to produce seeds! The following year he planted the survivor's seeds as well as those he'd acquired from seed swaps. Lofthouse wasn't concerned about specific varietal traits; he just wanted plants that could survive. In that second year some plants struggled and some did a little better. He saved seeds from the strongest. In year three he did the same, continuing to add new genetic material among the strongest from the previous year. In a very short time, Lofthouse was growing a patch of okra that was reaching 8 feet (2.4 m) tall and surviving the beginning of the frosty season. "Okra seems like one of the least inbred crops that I have worked with," he says. "The diversity within varieties is really pleasing to me. It gives lots of opportunity to select for vigor."

The idea of okra being a crop that is vigorous, is quickly adaptable, and features wide genetics is exciting in light of the climate challenges ahead. Food, and access to it, will be critical, and I believe that okra has the potential to feed a lot of people in a wide range of environments. Over the last few years I've taken to carrying a sign around with me at the various agricultural conferences I attend: I WANT TO TALK TO YOU ABOUT OKRA. Some people have stopped to talk to me, some people have looked at me funny, and some people have smirked, "Ew, I hate okra."

Only once a person approached me and said: "You want to see my okra tattoo?" His name badge read MIKE TAMBOLI, and he was a farmer.

It turned out Mike loves okra. The tattoo was the first clue; our 30-minute conversation about okra was the second. He said okra was his best crop: productive, reliable, drought-tolerant. He was the only person at that conference who mentioned climate change, stating that okra was a great crop in light of the increasing intensity of extreme weather events that really affected farmers.

"Pain in the ass to pick, but the kids love to eat it raw," he told me.

Our conversation about children and climate change really stuck with me. Perhaps because I have two young daughters; perhaps because I read and write post-apocalyptic fiction; perhaps because I have an overactive imagination; perhaps because the climate is going to hell in a handcart. As the world moves toward resurgent racism, religious extremism, xenophobic politics, and monocultured food systems, I believe more than ever that we need to celebrate and embrace diversity, human and plant alike. In the words of one of my daughter's favorite cartoon characters, "It's time to be a hero."

"For our children," says Okra.

"For the future," I agree.

Raw Okra Salad. *Photograph courtesy of Peter Taylor.*

Raw Okra Salad from 1916

by the editor of "The Country Women's Corner"

As a fan of raw okra, I was excited when I found a 1912 menu from the Waldorf-Astoria in New York that listed okra salad.[15] And a 1905 *USDA Farmers' Bulletin* on okra includes an okra salad recipe where the pods are boiled, noting: "This is a most delightful summer salad, the okra being very cooling."[16]

The following recipe is based on a description found in an article published in "The Country Women's Corner" column of the *Troy (Alabama) Messenger* in 1916.[17] The author was unnamed, but she included other delights such as okra pie, lazy okra, and okra hot slaw. To maximize the okra quotient, when I prepared this dish I made the dressing okra-centric by swapping in roasted okra seed sea salt from Well Seasoned Table, my own okra-flower-infused vinegar (see page 117), and okra seed oil from Clay Oliver Farm.

SALAD

2 cups thinly sliced raw okra
1 cup diced tomatoes
1 cup chopped cucumbers
1–2 cups finely chopped onion

DRESSING

1 clove garlic
½ teaspoon salt
¼ teaspoon pepper
2 tablespoons vinegar
⅓ cup olive oil

Mix the salad ingredients thoroughly and chill before serving. To make the dressing, crush the garlic in a bowl, leaving only the juice; add the salt, pepper, and vinegar, and lastly the oil. As an optional step, drop in a piece of ice, and beat quickly and thoroughly to thicken the dressing into a velvety smoothness. Place in a cool place until needed.

Note: Most okra salad recipes recommend boiling the okra first—just a 1- to 3-minute blanching in boiling water. I assume the quick blanch was a trick to eliminate any spininess of the pods. I have tried the salad using boiled pods and raw pods and am still drawn to the crunch and texture of the raw pods (choose spineless).

Red Velvet. *Photograph courtesy of Peter Taylor.*

CHAPTER 3

Embracing the S-Word

I say let's stop fighting the mucilaginous vegetable. Let okra do [its] own magnificent thing, after all it's only doing what comes naturally.[1]

—JESSICA HARRIS, *Africooks*

The international depth of culinary okra is astounding. Okra pods are grown and eaten across India and Southeast Asia, Australia, Africa, the Middle East and Mediterranean Europe, South and Central America, and the southern United States. Each locale has their culinary traditions and recipes. Statistics from the Food and Agriculture Organization of the United Nations show that India produces dramatically more okra than any other country, over 6 million tons in 2014, followed by Nigeria producing 2 million. Third in line is Sudan producing just shy of 300,000 tons. The United States limps over the finish line in 21st position, producing just under 10,000 tons in 2014. I should note that in 2017 the US imported almost 50,000 tons of okra, both fresh and frozen. Most of these imports came from Mexico, Honduras, and the rest of Central America.[2]

While the South has always, in general, embraced okra, some regions of the country are largely unaware of it. And even in the South, most cooks don't stray beyond a handful of common recipes. Which is a shame because okra is so versatile: You can pickle, ferment, and dehydrate it—these are all technically ways to eat okra raw. You can fry, boil, bake, grill, and steam it. You can slice, mash, julienne, and dice it. You can bread, batter, marinate, and season it. You can curry, casserole, stir-fry, and stew it.

Okra clears its throat, a little too loudly.

"What about the S-word," says Okra.

"Spiny? South? Stir-fry?" I say.

"*The* S-word," says Okra.

"I mentioned that already," I say.

"You said we'd deal with it?" says Okra.

"Maybe later," I say.

"You're procrastinating," says Okra.

"Don't be silly," I say.

"Last chance," says Okra, with a Look. The look says: *I've been dragged across oceans; I've been maligned by millions.*

"So be it," I say.

Slim·y / ˈslīmē/

adj. (slim·i·er, slim·i·est) covered by or having the feel or consistency of slime: the thick, slimy mud | the walls were slimy with lichens.

inf. disgustingly immoral, dishonest, or obsequious: he was a slimy people-pleaser.[3]

It always comes back to slime.

A 1905 *USDA Farmers' Bulletin* states, "Okra when cooked in water or in a mixture with liquid may develop a mucilaginous consistency, which many persons especially like in this vegetable."[4] However, by 1949 the principal horticulturist of the USDA, Victor R. Boswell, assessed that "okra alone is generally considered too 'gooey,' or mucilaginous, to suit American tastes."[5] In 1951 the same Victor R. Boswell authored an updated *USDA Farmers' Bulletin* on okra; note the significant shift in tone from the 1905 edition: "When cooked 'straight' its mucilaginous properties do not suit most people."[6] In a 1974 USDA survey,[7] adults named okra as one of the three vegetables they liked least, and children rated it with the four they liked second least, citing the texture as being undesirable. And more recently, in 2007, AOL conducted an online survey of America's most hated foods and okra ranked sixth.[8] In the span of a century, okra has gone from "especially liked" to "most hated."

I recently stumbled across a forgotten jar of fermented okra pods in my basement. They had been down there for an entire year, and all the okra stereotypes existed in this jar to the power of 10. My discovery of that jar happened to coincide with reading Jessica Harris's *The Africa Cookbook*, in which she encourages okra eaters to embrace the slime. As I pulled a chunk of gooey okra from the jar, the slime stretched out like the "danglies" we used to spit onto the ceilings at school, watching them drip down and hoping they'd land on some innocent's head. *Embrace the slime*, I thought. Oysters are slimy and people pay good money to slurp those snot-balls from their shells, so why not 365-day fermented okra? *For research*, I thought. And gulped it down.

It tasted good, maybe even great. The chili pepper that had also spent a year in the jar, and the traditional spice mix of mustard and peppercorns, had all created a delicious homogeneous flavor. I persuaded Belle to try some and we called it love-okra because she could eat a chunk and I could eat a chunk and then we could slurp up the slime until we met with a kiss (not unlike the romantic scene from *Lady and the Tramp*—but with okra instead of spaghetti).

I'm not asking you to eat 365-day fermented okra (you can build up to that), but I am asking you to reframe the way you think about the slimy-okra cliché. First, because there are probably slimy things that you like to eat (be honest), so why single out okra? Second, because there are so many ways to eat okra without it being slimy: Y'all just don't know how to cook it properly. This is the battle cry of the okra-loving southerner, charging forward, okra flag raised high. As culinary anthropologist Vertamae Grosvenor once said of southern chef Edna Lewis: "Her recipe for Whipped Cornmeal and Okra is so good it will make you fall in love with the slimy vegetable you swore you couldn't stand."[9] (How to cook okra properly is the focus of my next chapter, "Pods of the Gods.")

It seems that many okra trauma stories have childhood origins. In *The Cooking Gene*, Michael Twitty recounted one such childhood experience: "Another black medieval torture was okra. In our next kitchen, I remember my grandmother forcing me to eat okra. And all I knew was that it was pinkish on the inside for some reason and snotty and viscous, and looked as if it was going to come alive at any point and have me for dinner. My mother encouraged me to have one bite, but I knew one bite would translate to four bites, so I refused as if I were being sent off to the gulag. Finally, I put a piece in my mouth and marched upstairs to bed, but not before I spat it out in the toilet. Heritage, my ass."[10]

I don't have my own childhood traumas to recount when it comes to okra, although I was a fussy eater well into my teenage years. Instead, I'm vicariously living through my three-year-old, Emily. She eats okra raw and pickled with no obvious signs of trauma, although one time she did stick her finger into the goo forming at the end of her freshly bitten pod. She looked up at me with her half-confused, half-inquisitive frown.

"What's that?" she asked, as if a slug had just hugged her finger.

It was a good question. Scientifically speaking, the slug hug is a water-soluble polysaccharide found in lots of different plants and some microorganisms. It is a useful tool for regulating moisture loss and part of the reason why okra can tolerate high temperatures. While okra mucilage is

Making Your Own Okra Cosmetics

Yang Guifei of China and Cleopatra of Egypt are both noted in history for their outstanding beauty, and that beauty has been attributed to their consumption of okra. While this claim is unsubstantiated internet knowledge, it's interesting that okra slime could be the next aloe vera for skin and hair care. You can buy okra skin care products online, and the cosmetics company Lush once carried an okra-extract hair product. Shalini Vadhera, author of *Passport to Beauty*, writes of a Zimbabwean tradition of using boiled and mashed okra pods as a hydrating face mask.[11]

I wanted to test out the Zimbabwean-inspired okra pod rehydrating face mask and invited Belle and Emily to attend a special spa session. I laid towels on the floor, turned the lights down low, and lit a candle infused with lavender. I promised foot massages if they'd both accept my experimental face mask. I kept the process for making the face mask very simple: about 1 pound (0.5 kg) of okra pods and some water!

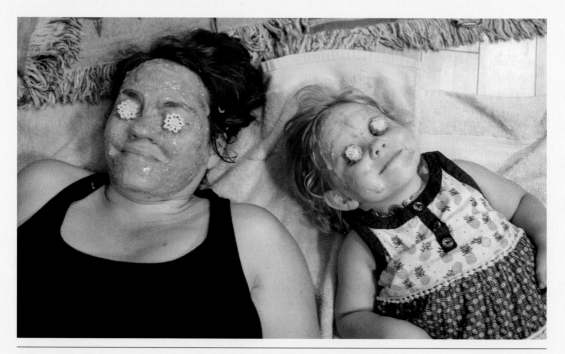

Belle and Emily are testing my unique homegrown organic okra spa treatment.

STEP 1. I selected pods that were not yet woody, figuring I was aiming for a smooth face mask and not an exfoliating one. (The older, woodier pods could work really well for making a body scrub.)

STEP 2. I placed the pods in a saucepan, covered them with water, and boiled them for 5 minutes to soften them up and make sure there was no residual spininess. Spa Treatment 101: Don't rub irritating trichomes into your loved one's face.

STEP 3. I poured the pods and the water into a blender and puréed them until the consistency seemed smooth and silky. The mixture bubbled green and gloopy and I felt like a witch over a cauldron.

STEP 4. I let the mixture cool to warm before applying. Having never been to spa school, I smeared the mask onto their faces with a silicon spatula while my subjects/patients/victims (you decide) lay with their eyes closed, eyelids covered with fresh slices of okra.

Here I am, using okra mucilage as a natural hydrating hair conditioner. *Photograph courtesy of Belle Crawford.*

Emily said it was nasty and didn't wait the suggested 5 minutes before washing it off, but Belle lay still for a good 10 minutes. She made only one complaint—when I accidentally pushed some slime up her nostril. (*Note*: Halloween applications: fake snot.) Afterward she said her skin felt awesome and asked me to put the rest of the okra slime in the fridge so she could use it again another day. Another popular cosmetic application is using okra slime as a hair product. Samantha Pollack's YouTube channel includes a video titled *Homemade Okra Conditioner for Natural Hair*. Pollack commented that her uncle in Suriname washes his dreadlocks with okra leaves. Now, I haven't used shampoo or conditioner on my hair in years, but I recently started swimming regularly and noticed how chlorine dries out my hair, so I decided to make myself the test subject for okra hair gel. I followed the same steps as for making the face mask, but instead of blending the pods I strained out the slime using cheesecloth to isolate just the mucilage. I massaged the gel into my hair and left it there for 15 minutes before rinsing. I'd say it worked well. Belle, who is a much better judge of hair than I am, said my hair felt and looked soft!

A Sweet Treat from Okra Slime

Okra slime's utility has parallels in another member of the Malvaceae family, *Althaea officinalis*, commonly known as marsh mallow. Marsh mallow is well known for its medicinal root extract, which was traditionally used (as its name suggests) to make marshmallows, but as with most members of the mallow family, its leaves and flowers are also edible. The medicinal applications include treatment of ulcers and sore throats and protection of respiratory health overall. Recent research shows that okra mucilage has a similar chemical composition to *Althaea officinalis* and could be used as a replacement.[12]

Katrina Blair's awesome book *The Wild Wisdom of Weeds* explores 13 common weeds for their medicinal and edible uses. One of those 13 is the common mallow, *Malva neglecta*. Blair makes mallow juice (blending the plant and then straining) and mallow water (steeping the roots and leaves in water) as daily tonics and the bases for many recipes. The alkalinizing, gut-cleansing, and joint-lubricating effects are powerful, and there is no reason that okra couldn't fill the same role and offer similar health benefits. Blair's book was full of inspiring ideas that I theorized could be applied to okra, so I contacted Blair and asked if she would be interested in adventuring in the world of okra marshmallows. I received a quick and enthusiastic yes, with a note that she'd seen some good-looking okra at her local farmers market.

It didn't take long for Blair to mail me a package of some of the first experimental okramallow treats. I had to fight off Belle and Emily to take a photograph of the gummy, green, honey-sweetened little rolls before they were consumed. Essentially, the confections were sweetened okra leather rolled in powdered cashews. I asked Blair whether there was a consensus opinion among her farmworkers, and she replied, "Delicious, with marshmallow consistency." Blair has called her creations Okra Marshmallow Delights (recipe at the end of this chapter). I think they have the consistency of Turkish delight, and the cashew powder reminds me of the powdered sugar on the boxed Turkish delight my siblings and I used to eat at Christmas when I was a child. One of my favorite okra varieties happens to be Yalova Akkoy from Turkey, which has been described as sweeter than other okras. I really want to make Blair's recipe using Yalova Akkoy pods so I can call them Turkish Okra Delights, but I'll have to wait until the next growing season.

the cause of much distaste, it has been researched for a wide range of useful applications, predominantly in the medical and food industries. Mucilage is not the same thing as mucus, but okra polysaccharides have been used to create mucoadhesive gels for nasal delivery of drugs, a natural alternative to the current synthetic options.[13] Further medical research has shown the okra gum to have antimicrobial properties effective against some bacterial strains. Of particular note: "An okra extract concentration of 97.7 mg/mL was completely effective in inhibiting bacterial growth. *S. aureus* can cause several illnesses from skin infections to pneumonia, meningitis and septicaemia and is the major cause of nosocomial infections worldwide, while *P. aeruginosa* is known for causing fatal lung infections in patients with cystic fibrosis."[14] When a friend cut her finger while helping me harvest okra, I advised her to rub some okra slime on it, and I wasn't entirely joking.

As early as the 1950s, researchers were investigating okra mucilage for use in blood plasma replacement. It was reported that a 2 percent okra plasma solution was administered to hemorrhaged dogs, which increased blood pressure and circulatory volume enough to keep them alive until the blood could be replaced.[15] Later work on the ability of okra mucilage to reduce fluid friction in turbulent flow linked in with the okra plasma, noting the potential to relieve turbulence in pathologically impacted sections of the circulatory system.[16] In the drug industry okra gum has been studied as a possible film coating for pills.[17]

Okra fiber for papermaking is discussed in chapter 9, but okra mucilage has also been used in the papermaking process. The John A. Manning Paper Company of Troy, New York, historically used a large quantity of Indian-sourced karaya gum in the manufacture of their paper. In the 1950s they began casting about for a replacement gum and commissioned an investigation into okra. Seven years of research led to the knowledge that okra gum was not only a suitable gum replacement, but actually a superior product. During the investigation a large number of spin-off food industry applications were explored, leading to the publication of a comprehensive report titled "Some Applications of Okra in the Food Industries."[18] The sheer quantity of useful applications of okra slime is quite exciting:

> *Okra powder has been used successfully as an emulsifying agent in mayonnaise and salad dressing where it acts as a protective colloid to preserve emulsion integrity. As a stabilizer, okra prevents the undesirable formation of ice crystals in ice cream and sherbets. It is used as a bodying agent in soups, gravies and related products; in these applications it also serves as a flavoring material. In cheese spreads okra gum acts as an emulsifier, which makes it possible to add water to make a creamy, smooth spread. In confectionery, okra is used in the formulation of fondants, frostings, sauces, etc. It controls the formation of large crystals and graininess, and it prevents the embrittlement of candy, such as fudge, when stored for long periods of time.*

Through work with the Marine Laboratory at the University of Miami, the same researcher also investigated the effect of okra mucilage as a preservative in the fish industry. He discovered that an okra-slime glaze and okra-slime ice improved the storage life of shrimp and prevented the development of malodorous smells (the slime's antimicrobial properties may account for this). Almost 60 years later a Brazilian researcher investigated using okra mucilage as a flexible and edible film.[19] This is part of a branch of research into active packaging, which aims to extend the shelf life of a product without artificial preservatives. She recognized that okra itself doesn't have a very long shelf life, and she is extracting mucilage from deteriorated okra pods to create the packaging that will improve okra's shelf life. That's a pretty awesome concept!

Within the food industry, okra mucilage has been subject to something called a pour test, which is exactly what you might imagine. A cup containing okra mucilage is tilted until the mucilage just begins to overflow. At that point the tilting is stopped and a measurement of how much liquid escapes the cup is taken. Adding acids, changing temperatures, or diluting the mucilage are ways to affect the viscosity as measured by the pour test. One study noted, "Okra mucilage solution, for example, behaves like egg white at higher concentrations forming threads and stabilizing foams, hence its use as a dried egg white substitute and extender has already been exploited."[20] Understanding the nature of the mucilage can be key to working with it in the kitchen, and manipulation of the slime through acidity, temperature, and dilution are all important tools.

In most cases the aim is slime reduction (fully explored in the next chapter). But embracing the slime is also a culinary option. The mucilage is contained *within* the cells of the okra pod and the seeds, so whole okra is not slimy. You can hold an okra pod in your hand and never feel like you're holding a slug . . . For slime lovers, cutting okra pods can be a wonderful release. Jessica Harris tells us, "Cutting the pod increases okra's 'sticking power' and some recipes from western Africa call for the pod to be minced into a gluey mass." I love using leftover black-eyed peas to cook Virginia Willis's Nigerian Black-Eyed Peas and Okra Fritters. This is a recipe that calls for mincing the okra and it definitely creates a gluey mass, with the mucilage binding all the ingredients together: onions, jalapeños, okra, and black-eyed peas. Vivian Howard's *Deep Run Roots* has a similar summer vegetable version with minced okra, corn, zucchini, and scallions. The slippery nature of the batter means you barely need to clean your fingers or the mixing container because the batter slides around the bowl. At one presentation I gave on okra, an elderly gentleman chuckled as he told me that they used to refer to okra as nature's Teflon. While I conceptually

OKRAVATIONS

Extracting Okra Slime

Slime is making somewhat of a positive impression thanks to the millennial YouTube phenomenon of glittery goo.[21] This "fun" slime is made of Elmer's Glue, borax, and water, but perhaps okra's slimy reputation can ride the wave of slime rebranded.

Extracting the slime from the pods is easy. Just follow this process.

Step 1. Gather overgrown pods that aren't good for eating anymore. You can use roots and leaves, too.

Step 2. Use a rolling pin to crush the pods. If you're using roots and leaves, chop them up.

Step 3. Place the crushed and chopped material in a bowl and cover with water. Let this sit for between 1 and 8 hours.

Step 4. Pour the liquid and vegetable matter through a colander or cheese-cloth. The liquid component will flow quite slowly, so allow time for it to drain out. If you're using cheesecloth, gather it around the vegetable matter and squeeze for maximum extraction.

Step 5. Use immediately or store in a jar in the fridge for about a week.

Belle and I were intrigued by Katrina Blair's description of the many benefits of mallow water in her book *The Wild Wisdom of Weeds*. It inspired us to start drinking straight-up okra slime as a daily internal moisturizer—it's kind of like drinking water with a personality.

"Err, hello?" says Okra.

"You should be a YouTube star," I say.

When dried okra rehydrates, it reclaims the classic okra slipperiness, so a regimen of okra slime for health and happiness can be carried through the winter and spring (more about that in chapter 5).

Crushing the pods and draining the slime.

understood what he was saying, I never really *got it* until I started making dishes like the Nigerian Fritters. They really put the *goo* in *good*. Timing is also important. Eating raw okra in the field with a swift bite-chew-swallow will leave you thinking okra isn't very slimy, but take a bite and luxuriously chew it for a few minutes and you'll have a very different experience.

I am often asked if I know of any low-slime okra varieties, and while I think the method of cooking is more important than the variety, I have come across some examples. Baker Creek Heirloom Seed Company advertises Eagle Pass as being low-slime, and Red Bowling has come up in conversations as being less slimy than other okras. The red varieties generally have a low-slime reputation. My personal hypothesis is that chunkier okra varieties with thicker pod walls are slimier, and many of the reds are thin-walled. The University of Ghana conducted a study on okra mucilage and noted that one of the chosen market varieties was a high-slime okra used by the Ewe tribe.[22] The Ewe word for "okra" is *fetri*, and traditional Ewe okra recipes tend to mince the okra pods into a slimy pulp. As do the Akan and Fanti people in Ghana. In *The Africa Cookbook*, Jessica Harris wrote: "The slime that has made it the most maligned of vegetables in this country, outside the South, is actually thought there [in Africa] to be a virtue." I say be brave, take the next step and embrace the S-word.

Okra Marshmallow Delights

by Katrina Blair

MAKES 15–20 PIECES

This creative recipe falls squarely into the you've-got-to-try-it-to-believe-it category. For anyone already familiar with Blair's book *The Wild Wisdom of Weeds*, that should come as no surprise. I have a mind to keep a stash of these perfectly sweet, deep green, chewy treats in my bag at all times so I can hand them out whenever someone tells me they don't like okra (which happens a lot). Katrina noted that the mixture tends to flatten out while dehydrating, which is why she created strips (a little like making fruit leathers) and formed the marshmallow shapes afterward. If you don't have a dehydrator, you could follow the same process using an oven at its lowest temperature setting; check regularly so the okra doesn't overcook. The aim is tacky-chewy, not hard-crunchy.

2 cups (200 g) sliced fresh okra
1 cup (225 ml) water, plus more
    if needed
½ cup (170 g) honey
2 tablespoons vanilla
½ cup (60 g) cashews,
    raw or roasted

Blend the okra with the water, honey, and vanilla in a high-powered blender until it creams up and becomes thick. Pour the mixture onto a dehydrator sheet in long strips and dry at 115°F (45°C) for about 6 hours. The mixture is dry enough once it can be peeled off the dehydrator sheet. Remove the strips from the sheet and tightly roll them up. The rolls can then be cut and formed into marshmallow-esque pieces. Powder the dry cashews in a food processer. Transfer the powder to a shallow bowl and roll the individual pieces in the powder until they appear white.

These marshmallow treats can be eaten raw or skewered on a stick and warmed over a fire.

Okra Marshmallow Delights.

Puerto Rico Evergreen. *Photograph courtesy of Peter Taylor.*

CHAPTER 4

Pods of the Gods

You talk of supping with the gods. You've just done it, for who but a god could have come up with the divine fact of okra.

—JAMES DICKEY, *Jericho* (1974)

I look upon this [okra] as the manna of the South, and I am only surprised that it is not more generally cultivated, cooked and eaten.

—*The Southern Planter* (1857)

Robb Walsh has been described as the Indiana Jones of food writing. He has traveled the world seeking out crazy, nasty, and weird things to eat. I'm a little saddened about the inclusion of okra in his book *Are You Really Going to Eat That?* But his chapter "Pods of the Gods" offers a somewhat redemptive experience with okra. The essay begins: "I was never much a fan of okra myself. Raising a forkful of the little green circles to my mouth and watching the slime drip away from the fork was usually enough to convince me that I didn't really want to put them in my mouth."

I am often asked how I respond when people tell me they don't like okra. In turn, I've asked many people that question as I worked on this book. Virginia Willis hit the nail on the head, saying, "Those who hate it think it's slimy, gooey, and gummy. In my opinion, they just haven't met the right okra."

The question then becomes: How do I help you meet the right okra? And while the answer can be somewhat subjective, I believe there is an okra out there for everyone. Eating okra raw wins over a lot of people, for example—there is a grassy sweetness to the pods, and the satisfying feeling of healthiness and well-being from consuming something crunchy and green. When it comes to cooking the pods, there are three main themes behind the myriad preparations: pairing with acid, high-heat cooking, and diluting with water. You may remember these from the last chapter as being the three principal ways to manipulate mucilage.

Okra Plus Acid

The person to introduce Robb Walsh to the right okra was Dot Hewitt, a celebrated chef from Austin, Texas. Hewitt was well known and loved for simple but excellent food that always remained southern and affordable. The "right" okra turned out to be stewed okra and tomatoes, and here is what Walsh learned from Dot Hewitt: "Don't cut the okra. Don't boil the okra. Just rinse off the pods and stew them in tomato sauce. If you give it a chance, it will change your mind about okra." This pairing of okra and tomatoes is a useful combination in the kitchen because, as summer crops, they produce in abundance at around the same time (July and August are peak production times in the Southeast). This is reflected in the panoply of okra-tomato recipes you'll find if you start looking: stewed okra and tomatoes; okra and tomato soup; sautéed okra and tomatoes; gumbo; succotash; roasted okra and tomatoes; southern ratatouille; Brunswick stew; and so on. The trend is also reflected in most okra-eating regions. In the Middle East we see meat (often beef) and *bamia* stewed with tomatoes; India has Bhindi Masala, tomato bhindi sabzi, and a whole host of okra-tomato variations; a West African *gombo* sauce is basically just okra, tomatoes, and chilies; gini-sang okra from the Philippines is sautéed okra with pork, but includes tomatoes; Zeytinyağlı *bamya* is a Turkish dish that is okra in olive oil with onions and tomatoes and peppers; and the list goes on.

The combination is based on more than just commonality of seasons, though—you won't find recipe after recipe pairing okra and zucchini. The secret is that the acidity of the tomatoes cuts through the mucilage. You can test this yourself by taking two jars of okra slime, adding apple cider vinegar to one (acidic) and baking soda to the other (alkaline), and observing how the viscosity changes. Add any acid when cooking okra—tomatoes, lemon juice, or vinegar—and you'll end up with a less slimy dish. This means okra slime-reduction cooking can be as simple and delicious as throwing some okra pods and chopped tomatoes in a roasting pan with a little salt and pepper or Cajun seasoning and baking it all on medium-high for 30–40 minutes. Or life can be as complicated as Brunswick stew.

Brunswick stew may have originated in Brunswick, Virginia, or Brunswick, Georgia, but both places offer up a dish that combines a tomato base, mixed local vegetables, and small wild game (rabbit, squirrel, or the like).

My brother says I'm lucky, but I like to think I throw ideas into the universe with open-minded optimism and the universe responds. Either way it came as no great surprise to me when, just days after I came across a Brunswick stew recipe from a 1906 cookbook, a suicidal squirrel threw itself under my truck. I diligently swung the truck around, pulled up alongside the squirrel, and delighted in the fact that I'd merely clipped its head. A perfect roadkill specimen. With squirrel in truck, I headed home and Googled *skinning a squirrel* while simultaneously rereading *Woods Lore and Wildwoods Wisdom*, a book by local legendary woodsman Doug Elliott. To stand on a squirrel's tail and pull on its hind legs, gently but firmly peeling the skin off and inside out (like removing a very tight sock) is both grotesque and fascinating, but mainly grotesque. With the squirrel skinned and gutted and slowly cooking in the Crock-Pot, I consulted Belle.

"How do you feel about okra and squirrel stew?" I asked.

"Hell no," she said.

I'm still not forgiven for trying to skin a squirrel in the kitchen sink, but I offer the venerable recipe in case you want to channel your energy into running over a squirrel. (If you get one I suggest you avoid possible eviction by an angry spouse and just skin it outside.)

> *Clean and cut up 4 squirrels as for a fricassee. Put over the fire in a saucepan with an onion chopped fine, just enough boiling water to cover, and a high seasoning of salt and pepper. Cover and stew slowly until the meat is very tender. Partly cool and remove as many of the bones as possible. Return to the fire with 1 quart of tomatoes, 1 pint of green corn cut from the cob, ½ pint of lima beans, 1 pint of diced white potatoes, 1 diced cucumber, 1 diced small white summer squash, 1 diced carrot, and a scant pint of sliced okra. Add 1 tablespoonful of butter and more seasoning and stew for 2 hours longer, or until the vegetables are cooked to pieces.[1]*

My own contribution to the world of okra and tomatoes is okra pizza. I've recently (and reluctantly) given up dairy, but have found that grilled vegetables on thinly baked bread with a tomato sauce tastes really good (I try not to think of it as pizza, because cheese).

"It's the aged mammary excretion of cows," says Okra.

"Correction: It's the *delicious* aged mammary excretion of cows."

Slicing the okra lengthwise and embedding them, seeds down, in the tomato sauce is aesthetically pleasing and allows the bottom edge of the okra pods to stew a little while the top roasts. It's really good; I've even thrown

Livening up a frozen pizza with a few strips of okra!

okra on a frozen cheese pizza for my family and they've gobbled it up. If you're making your own crust, try substituting a small amount of ground roasted okra seeds (see "Making Your Own Okra Seed Flour," page 154, for roasting instructions) in the dough mix for a little flour diversity and flavor.

Some recipes call for an acidic pre-treatment to add extra heft in the war against slime. Soaking the whole pods in vinegar or marinating in citrus prior to cooking does help. Okra pickles (which I describe in the next chapter) are likely popular because they are basically okra soaked in vinegar, which means less slime. In a *Washington Post* article, food writer Emily Horton explored some common slime-cutting methods and noted that acidic treatments are not perfect at cutting out the slime, but are much better than no treatments.[2]

Okra Plus Water

Everything about okra is slime this and slime that until we get to gumbo. As soon as the topic of gumbo comes up, there is a switch in terminology and suddenly we're praising okra's magical thickening effect. It's bad until we want it and then it's good. A quick look at gumbo recipes shows a wide variety of versions and ingredients being employed, including meats, seafood, and thickeners. Okra doesn't even need to be included for a dish to be called gumbo. In *New Orleans Cuisine* contributor Cynthia LeJeune Nobles wrote, "Today's purists still insist that there are only two types of gumbo, okra and filé—period. Those desiring more nuances classify it into three broad categories, Creole Gumbo, Cajun Gumbo, and Gumbo Z'Herbes, then subcategorize it into Gumbo Fevis (okra gumbo), Gumbo Filé, or plain roux gumbo, and then break it down at least a dozen times more according to the main ingredients."[3] That purist definition of filé gumbo or fevi gumbo is reflected in writing as far back as 1788.[4] Filé is the powdered leaf of the sassafras tree, a native of North America, with thickening effects similar to okra's. *Fevi* is a Creole term for "okra" or "okra gumbo."[5] Today the use of filé (sassafras powder) and fevi (okra) is still a distinguishing part of modern gumbo dishes, with an unwritten rule that either can be used but never together. I discovered that the rule is sometimes broken when I came across a jar of premade "gumbo" that boasted on its label, THE TRINITY OF GUMBO: FILÉ, FEVI AND ROUX. (Buying a jar of gumbo likely breaks some other gumbo rules, too.) The use of a roux to thicken and darken gumbo was a later development that came to define many Gulf Coast gumbos.

The predecessor to gumbo was okra soup, and we've already seen that the word *gumbo* has etymological roots in many of the Bantu languages of West Africa (Kimbundu, *kingombo*; Samba, *goombo*; Ngong, *kengombo*; Mbuun, *ingombo*).[6] The origin of okra soup also has clear ties to West Africa, most famously in Senegal's soupikandia, an okra-thickened soupy stew.[7] This is not surprising, since the entire 3,500-mile (5,633 km) coastline of West Africa was heavily exploited by the transatlantic slave trade. The foods and culinary traditions of the people trafficked along the Middle Passage shaped the African Diaspora. Okra soup as prepared by enslaved cooks was quickly adopted into the food culture of the South and became highly praised, especially in the Low Country. It shows up on menus and in cookbooks throughout the 1800s.

As okra became more popular, it was adopted into many regional dishes. Jessica Harris wrote, "In the South, where enslavement lasted longer and climate made Africans and their descendants most at home, it [okra] is revered and treated with respect. It's an ingredient in the southern succotashes of many states and reigns supreme in many of the gumbos of New Orleans and southern Louisiana. Southerners just seem to know (or perhaps have learned from African Americans) how to savor the slippery juice that the tender pods exude when they are cut."[8]

Michael Twitty added to the list: "Some varieties of Kentucky burgoo and the Brunswick stew of the Southeastern coast contain bits of okra thrown in with the usual mix of tomatoes, onions and hot pepper. Okra soup thick with crab became Baltimore's 'crab gumbo' and Charleston and Savannah's 'rouxless gumbo,' while in New Orleans the roux made okra soup even thicker. Summer Louisiana gumbo came to mean okra gumbo flavored with chicken, seafood or whatever the seasons allowed."[9]

When okra began to show up in the early receipt books, it was as okra soup. Mary Randolph's *The Virginia Housewife* included a recipe for "Ochra Soup," published in 1824. She also has a recipe for "Gumbo—A West India Dish," which is basically geographically misplaced boiled okra. Mrs. Lettice Bryan's *The Kentucky Housewife* also included an okra soup and a gumbo recipe, published in 1885. In that era southern white women were surrounded by enslaved black cooks who were prevented from learning to read and write, and these early recipes are clearly the creations of those cooks, although no attribution is given.

In 1831 John Legare, Charleston editor of *The Southern Agriculturist*, responded to a request of the *Genesee Farmer* (a New York–based magazine) to provide instructions on preparing okra soup:

> *This fine vegetable appears nowhere to be so justly appreci-*
> *ated as in the neighborhood of Charleston—here it furnishes a*
> *portion of the daily food of, we believe, at least, three-fourths*
> *of the inhabitants of the city during the season. In fact, we*
> *know of no vegetable which is so generally used by both rich*
> *and poor, or which so justly merits the encomiums bestowed*
> *on it. When served up, simply boiled, we admit it is not the*
> *most palatable vegetable we ever eat, but in the form of soup*
> *well boiled, with a proper supply of tomatoes, etc., we doubt*
> *whether it is excelled by any other in the world, either in fla-*
> *vor, wholesomeness, or nutriment.*[10]

While modern roux-based gumbo is distinct from Legare's recipe for okra soup, the historic connection is at risk of being lost, or worse, disregarded with alternative origins. "As the green, finger-shaped vegetable pops up on menus across the United States as an emblem of Southern American cooking, the true narrative of the plant is at risk of disappearing," Harris has said.[11] The dispute is seen as part of a wider denial of the influence of the enslaved Africans and African food on American food culture.

There are two counter-narratives regarding the origins of gumbo. First is the argument that gumbo evolved from a French dish called bouillabaisse, which is a fish-based stew. This appears to be a wholly Eurocentric myth. In an essay titled "The Origin Myth of New Orleans Cuisine," food historian Lolis Eric Elie wrote, "As for the relationship between gumbo and bouillabaisse, I can find very little."[12] I also spoke with Dr. Shane Bernard, a Louisiana author and historian, about gumbo. Bernard pointed to the earliest written reference to gumbo, from a court document that details part of the interrogation of an enslaved person about allegations of theft.[13] In the transcript, the interrogator references "un gombeau." Dr. Bernard noted, "The significance of this passage is that it pushes back the earliest known reference to gumbo to 1764—indicating that the dish was known in Louisiana even before the arrival of the Acadian exiles, whose Cajun descendants (unjustly or not) are the ethnic group most often associated with gumbo by the general public."

The second narrative is less clear. It suggests that gumbo has its origins in the Native American use of filé to thicken stews. It is clear that European settlers integrated the food cultures of both Native Americans and enslaved Africans, and the Choctaw word for "filé" is *kombo*, which could be an alternative etymology of the word *gumbo*. However, multiple early references to gumbo as both a thickened soup and a plant (okra) make me think that gumbo is more clearly linked to okra than sassafras. Perhaps sassafras was first used as a winter alternative, or developed as an individual stew that later melded with the okra preparation and assumed the same name.

Okra Plus Heat

According to my I-want-to-talk-to-you-about-okra research, grilled okra comes up as the number one okra converter. Take medium-sized whole pods, brush with a little olive oil or okra seed oil (see chapter 9 for more about okra seed oil), and sprinkle with salt, pepper, or some Cajun seasoning. Grill on high heat until the pods begin to brown on each side and serve hot with a generous squeeze of fresh lime. Throw in a spicy mayonnaise dip and these tender, no-slime pods will have people questioning their anti-okra convictions. The light charring brings out the underlying sweetness of the pods, and the lime really takes this dish from good to awesome. I think that's in part due to the pairing of flavors, but the acidity of the lime may also balance out some of the residual slimy textures. On top of all those flavors is the slime-reducing nature of high-heat preparations.

Jeanne Osnas and Katherine Preston are PhD plant ecologists and evolutionary biologists who run the website *Botanist in the Kitchen*. They explore the botany behind cooking, and anyone who pairs chocolate (a red chili mole sauce) with fried okra is well worth paying attention to! With regard to okra, they note, "Heating over 90°C (close to boiling) reduces viscosity even when the dish is cooled again, probably because it denatures some associated proteins."[14] A Malaysian research study tested the viscosity of okra mucilage at different temperatures, and their results corroborate the kitchen experience, demonstrating declining viscosity with increasing temperatures.[15] This is contrary to some touted okra knowledge that suggests heating okra increases the viscosity, but I think this misinformed concept is extrapolated from okra's use as a thickening agent in soups and gumbos. Cooking in water will always result in lower temperatures than cooking in oil, so soups and gumbos are a more favorable environment for mucilage to persist and thicken the dish. This means that frying okra is a legitimate way to reduce the slime content.

There are many who will tell you that the only way to eat okra is fried. It is certainly the way many people are introduced to okra, probably as a side at BBQ joints or southern diners. Perhaps as part of a family tradition in summer, when okra is podding in the garden or the farmers markets start selling. Pre-breaded frozen okra ready for dumping in the fryer is available year-round. Having grown up in England, where you can buy deep-fried Mars Bars at your local fish-and-chip shop, I'm convinced people will eat anything if it's deep-fried. Garden writer Felder Rushing confirms that deep-fried addictions are not just a British thing. He once told me, "I love growing okra—mostly 'Burgundy'—as an unkillable summer mallow, but the main way I eat it is fried, with ketchup. But then, being a Southerner, I'd probably eat fried ketchup."

There are many ways to fry okra, but when people (southerners) talk about fried okra they speak to a certain preparation of sliced pods rolled in meal and deep-fried. Within that description there are still many variations and nuances and family recipes and *my grandmother makes the best . . .* One person I spoke to told me their family recipe was two parts cornmeal and one part flour, as passed down from their great-grandmother who was born in 1863. In 1857 *The Southern Planter* journal offered this advice: "Okra is very good fried. Cut into thin slices and fry in lard or butter."[16] You can't get much simpler than that! Menus listing fried okra increased in the early 1900s, which coincides with the industrialization of the cooking oil industry. In 1930 the Bureau of Home Economics published a recipe for a simple fried okra (not breaded) with the commentary that okra was becoming more popular across the United States.[17] Today the iconic light-golden-with-glimpses-of-green, barrel-esque, bite-sized treat is likely the most popular way people consume okra.

Ron Cook, the Heavy Hitter okra breeder from Oklahoma, told me, "One year, the chefs at the new Cherokee Nation Casino came here to pick all the fixins for the official state meal from my garden. They were hosting a legislative dinner and wanted food grown locally. Otherwise, I wouldn't even know that Oklahoma had a state meal." The official state meal of Oklahoma was designated in 1988 and comprises fried okra, corn bread, barbecued pork, squash, biscuits, sausage and gravy, grits, corn, strawberries (state fruit), chicken-fried steak, pecan pie, and black-eyed peas.

"Okrahoma," I joked to Ron.

He ignored me. I guessed it was an overused joke, but I still thought it was pretty funny.

"Mediokra!" says Okra.

If this has set you to wondering what your state's State Meal is, let me save you the trouble. Unless you live in Oklahoma or Louisiana, you don't have one. And technically Louisiana has a designated State Cuisine (gumbo, 2014) and then a separate North Louisiana Meal (a long list of items, including fried okra, 2015). In related state-inspired pub quiz okra factoids: An annual Okra Strut in Irmo, South Carolina, features a giant inflatable okra; Burkville, Alabama, hosts an annual Okra Festival with an okra-eating contest; Galveston, Texas, has an annual Okrafest with themed cocktails; and Checotah, Oklahoma, had an annual Okrafest for 15 years, but it stopped running in 2010. Texas appears to be the only state to inspire okra-based fiction. A chick-lit novel, *The Goddess of Fried Okra*, sees the heroine of the story traveling across Texas while learning swordplay and how to cook the best fried okra. On the way she discovers her true inner value. Perhaps Okra is on a similar narrative arc, a journey of self-discovery that will end in a full realization of its potential, and a sword fight.

Delta State University claims the most aggressive (nonfictional) okra. Their official mascot is a Statesman, but students comically adopted a personified okra wearing boxing gloves because a "Statesman wasn't very frightening." In the mid-1990s a student vote adopted the Fighting Okra as the university's unofficial mascot. The Delta State website reports: "Despite some rowdy student objections, athletic programs at Delta State University do not use the student-chosen sub-mascot, Fighting Okra. The Fighting Okra, the most vicious of all vegetables, was created by a band of students at DSU in the late 1980s and early 1990s. While some on campus embrace the scary veggie, DSU Athletics does not."

◉ ◉ ◉

When I give presentations on okra in the Asheville area, if I don't mention it first, someone is guaranteed to bring up Chai Pani, a local Indian street-food restaurant. Usually the comment goes along the lines of, "Have you ever tried the okra fries at Chai Pani?" Usually their eyes are glistening with the joyful memory, or audible swallowing lets me know their salivary glands are having a Pavlovian reaction. The fries really are delicious. I've been enjoying them since well before I first talked with James Beard Award–winning chef Meherwan Irani and learned the story behind them.

"Almost everyone that comes to Chai Pani orders the okra," said Irani. "Can that be said of any other southern restaurant? We go through an average of 15 bushels a day."

That's almost 400 pounds (181 kg) of okra!

"Originally I wanted it to be a seasonal dish so we could source locally grown okra, but people come from all over expecting to try the okra fries. In season we source locally at around $20 a case, but out of season we bring okra in from Central America at $40–50 a case. What can you do? It's become our signature dish."

Irani was born in England but grew up in India, near Mumbai, and I was amused to learn that okra-induced childhood trauma is not limited to the United States. "Lady's Fingers [okra] flourishes in India and is universally hated by children," he told me.

He went on to explain that okra is an abundant and affordable vegetable in India and so his mother would cook it a lot, ignoring the complaints of Irani and his brother. But one day his mother did something different. "We were eating outside and it was hot, real Indian heat. My mother came out carrying a bowl lined with paper towels and filled with these thin strips of deep fried okra. My brother and I tried some and we loved it. In all my childhood I think we only had okra prepared that way two or three more times—oil was still an expensive luxury in India—but I'll never forget that first experience."

Fast-forward to 2009 when Irani was opening Chai Pani. He wanted to create authentic Indian food, but he also wanted his menu to have a sense of its southern locale. The menu includes dishes such as kale pakoras and ingredients like sweet potatoes and squash.

"One day I was in a mom-and-pop-type restaurant and I saw fried okra on the menu. I ordered it on a whim and it was ghastly! The breading was saturated with oil and the okra inside was still slimy."

Irani's okra experience was an exact replica of the first time I'd tried okra in 2006. The difference is that for Irani it sparked an epiphany that seems so obvious in the retelling, but had evaded him until that moment.

"I immediately phoned my mother," Irani told me. "What was her secret? What had made her okra so special?"

It turns out there's nothing special about Irani's mother's fried okra at all. It is splendid simplicity, not even a secret. Just four ingredients: okra, salt, lime, and oil. Julienne lengthwise, deep-fry, add lime and salt, and toss to coat.

"I give full credit to my mother," said Irani. "I think the true genius, the two things that make these fries so good, comes from the lime and cutting the pods lengthwise like shoestring fries."

Speaking with Irani reminded me of a passage from John T. Edge's *Potlikker Papers*: "Southern food has never been static. Like all expressions of culture, from music to literature, foodways have been fluid reflections of time and place . . . By the 2010s, second generation blendings of cultures proved essential in the making of the newest New South, in which expertise in tortilla making mattered as much as biscuit making, and Indian chefs set the standard for fried okra."

I always order the okra fries at Chai Pani and I'll happily order fried okra as a side in any decent southern restaurant (those that cut and bread the okra themselves and don't simply pour a bag of frozen pre-breaded okra into a deep fryer and call it good), but I never deep-fry things at home. I like to shallow-fry and oven-roast, but deep-frying requires too much oil and effort. That doesn't mean the world of fried okra is lost to me, though. I shallow-fry young whole okra pods for just a few minutes on each side. The pods take on a bright emerald glow, and the Chai Pani salt-and-a-lime trick has them disappearing from the table before they have a chance to cool and dull. When I slice and bread okra to shallow-fry it, I create something that is more reminiscent of Vivian Howard's recipe for Okra Hash from her book *Deep Run Roots*. For Vivian Howard, this is a recipe remembered from childhood: "Ms. Linda's was a mix of textures and degrees of doneness I never got enough of. She sliced them into little rounds. Some were completely shrouded in salty cornmeal and perfectly crisp; other pieces were slightly too dark and kind of nutty. And a little bit in every serving was naked, kissed only by cast-iron, oil, and salt."

Another home-based "frying" option is the air fryer. I must admit that I had no idea what an air fryer was until I was visiting some friends in California who had never eaten okra. Obviously I had to lessen their ignorance, and so I brought okra to a family cookout. My intention had been to grill it (remember: number one okra converter), but then I was introduced to the air fryer. It's a small superheated convection oven that creates a fried-like effect without all the oil. We sliced the okra, mixed it with a little olive oil and garlic salt, "fried" it for 4 minutes at 450°F (230°C), and enjoyed a perfectly delicious okra snack (a squirt of lime juice completed the dish). They told their four-year-old it was "special asparagus" and she loved it, bringing us one step closer to chef Virginia Willis's vision: "I like to think of it as the next asparagus. It's only a matter of time before the love of okra spreads." Willis included multiple fried okra recipes in her *Okra* cookbook, including Crispy Greek Fried Okra, Indian Fried Okra with Spiced Yogurt, and many southern versions. She noted that researching recipes for the book led her to realize that "every culture that utilizes okra in its cuisine has a fried okra recipe."

My contribution to the world of fried okra is a dish I call All-Star Okra. I like to pick an okra variety like Star of David or Perkins Spineless with deeply ridged pods that provide lots of surface area to capture the flour. I slice the pods crosswise into ¼-inch (6 mm) segments; the star-like cross section of the deep-ridged varieties gives the recipe its name. I dry-fry these stars in a cast-iron skillet until they begin to blacken, allow them to cool slightly, and then dip them in whisked egg. Next I mix the egg-covered stars with okra seed meal (see "Making Your Own Okra Seed Flour," page 154) and shallow-fry them in okra seed oil. Serve hot and garnish with a fresh okra flower to complete the All-Star Okra dish.

"I'm an all-star!" says Okra.

Limpin' Susan

by Chef BJ Dennis

SERVES 4–6

Limpin' Susan has often been called the wife (or sometimes cousin) of Hoppin' John, the more famous dish of peas and rice traditionally made on New Year's Day to ensure wealth and good luck for the coming year. Like Hoppin' John, there are many variations of Limpin' Susan, but they always include rice, shrimp, and okra, and often bacon. Gullah Geechee chef BJ Dennis shares this as a classic Charleston dish. In the Low Country and the Sea Islands, Limpin' Susan is classically served over rice.

Peanut oil (or other favorite oil)
1½ pounds (680 g) okra, sliced
1 pound (453 g) shrimp, peeled
¼ pound (113 g) bacon, cooked and diced (optional)
2–3 teaspoons minced garlic
1 teaspoon minced chili pepper
1 teaspoon minced ginger
½ onion, diced
Kosher salt and black pepper, to taste
Minced parsley, to taste
Minced thyme, to taste

Place a 10-inch (25 cm) cast-iron skillet over medium heat and add just enough oil to coat the bottom. Add the okra and cook until it begins to brown, stirring occasionally. (If the okra starts to stick, add more oil.) Add the next six ingredients, season with salt and pepper, and cook 5 minutes. Add the herbs to the skillet and cook until shrimp is ready, 2 to 3 minutes more. If desired, add more salt and pepper.

Limpin' Susan. *Prepared by chef Stephen Goff, photograph courtesy of Peter Taylor.*

Bhindi Masala

by Chef Meherwan Irani

SERVES 4–6

This is a traditional okra (bhindi) dish from Maharashtrian, the Indian state where chef Irani grew up. Irani told me that okra slime is as disliked in India as in the US, and his top tip for avoiding okra's "characteristic gummi-ness" is to pre-fry the sliced okra so it starts off a little crispy. One of the joys of cooking Indian food is the aromas of all the spices. Fresh spices are so important that Irani started his own spice company (Spicewalla), which sources high-quality ingredients from around the world. Irani also noted that Roma tomatoes work well with Bhindi Masala, but said, "I like crushed tomatoes because they're usually vine ripened and have more flavor in cooking. You can get high quality and organic tomatoes in a can just about anywhere." A final word of warning when frying the onions: Watch them closely—the onions can change from brown to burnt very quickly.

1 cup (250 ml) canola oil
2 pounds (907 g) okra, cut into
    small rounds
2 teaspoons cumin seeds
1 serrano pepper, diced (or 2 for a
    spicier flavor)
1 small red onion, diced
1 teaspoon kosher salt
2 tablespoons ginger garlic paste
1 teaspoon red chili powder
1 teaspoon turmeric powder
1 teaspoon cumin powder
1 teaspoon coriander powder
    (optional)
½ cup (8 g) chopped cilantro
1 small can (13.5 fl. oz. / 398 ml)
    crushed tomatoes, or 2 large
    fresh tomatoes, diced
½ teaspoon sugar

Heat the oil in a saucepan. In small batches, fry the okra rounds until the edges are browned (3–4 minutes) and transfer with a slotted spoon to a paper napkin. Place ¼ cup (60 ml) of the frying oil in a wide-bottomed pan over medium-high heat. Add the cumin seeds. Wait about half a minute and add the diced serrano peppers. Next, within 1 minute, add the onion with the salt (the salt helps the onion cook more quickly by drawing out the moisture). When the onion starts to lightly brown, add the ginger garlic paste and cook on medium heat until the onion starts turning completely brown.

Add the powders (red chili, turmeric, cumin, coriander). When they start to clump together with the onion, add half the cilantro and ¼ cup (60 ml) water. The water helps deglaze the pan; stir and scrape to get all the fond (good stuff) off the bottom of the pan. The spices cook quickly so this process should take only 2–3 minutes. Once the water has evaporated, add the tomatoes and sugar. Cook the tomatoes on medium for 10 minutes or so, until they are completely broken down and the mixture looks glossy. Add the fried okra, mixing gently (so that the okra doesn't break down) until the okra is hot. Taste for salt and garnish with the rest of the fresh cilantro. Serve over rice with warm roti, paratha, or even toasted crusty bread.

Bhindi Masala. *Prepared by chef Jamie Swofford, photograph courtesy of Peter Taylor.*

FOR THE GINGER GARLIC PASTE. Blend approximately 4 tablespoons peeled garlic and 4 tablespoons peeled fresh ginger into a smooth paste in a food processor—a teaspoon of oil will help it blend smoothly. The leftover paste will keep refrigerated in a glass jar for at least a month, but it rarely lasts that long! This stuff is gold—it makes a great base rub on chicken and meats. If you don't have a food processor, finely mince a tablespoon of ginger and garlic and mix together.

Spicy Okra

by Chef Marcus Samuelsson

SERVES 4–6

I am pleased to include a recipe from Ethiopia because okra has its origins there. Chef Marcus Samuelsson has many culinary influences. Born in Ethiopia, Samuelsson was adopted by and grew up in a Swedish family in Gothenburg. He now lives and cooks in New York City. You can see the Ethiopian influence in this recipe (from his book *The Soul of a New Cuisine*), which has similarities to the traditional Ethiopian okra dish Bamya Alicha. Samuelsson says this about the dish:

> *People tend to either love or hate okra, which originated in Africa and spread to Arabia, Europe, the Caribbean, Brazil, India, and the United States. I happen to love it and think it adds great texture and color to meals, but I do remember being a little put off by its slimy texture the first time I had it. Once you get over that, it's easy to like. Look for pods that are uniform in color, with no discoloration or soft spots. Smaller pods are usually more tender than large pods.*

1½ pounds (680 g) okra, cut into 1-inch (2.5 cm) pieces
2 tablespoons peanut oil
2 medium red onions, sliced
4 tomatoes, chopped
2 bird's-eye chilies, seeds and ribs removed, chopped
½ cup (60 g) peanuts, coarsely chopped
3 cloves garlic, minced
½ teaspoon salt, or to taste

Bring a medium saucepan of salted water to a boil. Add the okra and simmer until tender, about 5 minutes. Drain and pat dry.

Heat the oil in a large sauté pan over high heat. Add the onions, tomatoes, chilies, and peanuts; sauté, stirring frequently, until the onions are translucent, about 5 minutes. Reduce the heat to medium, add the garlic, and cook until golden, about 5 minutes. Stir in the okra and cook until heated through, about 2 minutes. Season with the salt.

Spicy Okra. *Prepared by chef Jamie Swofford, photograph courtesy of Peter Taylor.*

Okra Fries

by Chef Vivian Howard

SERVES 4

This recipe likely wins the most cooked recipe award in my kitchen. It is quick and easy and consistently delicious. My daughter loves it, guests love it, and I love it. That said, all of the okra recipes from Howard's book *Deep Run Roots* are pretty awesome.

Here is her introduction to the okra fries:

Okra cooked in the oven like this are a revelation. The first time I did it, I planned on having them as a side with dinner, but I ate every single piece before we sat down and concluded they were more appropriate as a snack. In the spirit of kale chips, but way tastier and more substantial, these fries will cook unevenly, so expect some crispy spots mingled with more chewy bites. If you're using large, fat okra, slice them into quarters. If you've got immature pods, split them in half.

1 pound okra (453 g; 20–25 pods), split or quartered lengthwise
2 tablespoons extra-virgin olive oil
2 teaspoons ground coriander
1 teaspoon salt
10 turns of the pepper mill or ¼ teaspoon black pepper

Preheat the oven to 400°F (200°C). In a medium bowl, toss the okra with the olive oil, coriander, salt, and black pepper. Spread the okra onto a large baking pan, or two pans if necessary. What's important is that the okra have plenty of room to spread out. If they are all piled on top of one another, they will steam, not roast. Slide the pan onto the middle rack of the preheated oven. After 10 minutes, toss the okra gently with a spatula and rotate the pans if you are using two. Cook an additional 10 to 15 minutes. When the okra is done, it will be brown and crispy in a lot of places but shouldn't smell burnt. Serve warm or at room temperature as a snack.

Okra Fries. *Photograph courtesy of Peter Taylor.*

Round Steak and Okra Gumbo

by Chef Virginia Willis

There are likely as many gumbo recipes out there as there are southern chefs, but when Louisiana-born chef Virginia Willis told me this was a favorite from her book *Okra*, I knew I had to include it. Here is her introduction to the gumbo:

> *Round steak is the cut of beef most often used for country-fried steak in the South. It's from the back leg of a cow, is quite lean, and can be very tough. It's often sold as steaks and little less than ½ inch thick. Even though I grew up eating gumbo in Louisiana, I wasn't familiar with beef gumbo until I started research for my book. This recipe is old-fashioned country cooking—inexpensive, filling, and really, really good.*

1 pound (453 g) beef round steak, sliced into 1-inch (2.5 cm) strips

Coarse kosher salt and freshly ground black pepper

4 tablespoons canola oil, divided

1 medium slice ham steak, about ½ inch (1.3 cm) thick, diced

2 tablespoons all-purpose flour

1 onion, finely chopped

1 quart (950 ml) homemade beef stock or reduced-fat, low-sodium beef broth, heated

1 pound (453 g) okra, stem ends trimmed, finely chopped

Season the round steak with salt and pepper. Heat 2 tablespoons of the oil in a large heavy-bottomed pot until shimmering. Add the steak and ham. Cook until the steak is browned on both sides, 2 to 2½ minutes per side. Using a slotted spoon, remove the steak and ham to a plate.

Add the remaining 2 tablespoons of oil to the drippings in the pot. Add the flour and stir to combine. Cook until brown, about 5 minutes. Add the onion and cook until soft and translucent, 3–5 minutes. Return the browned meats to the pan and stir to combine. Then add the stock and okra and season with salt and pepper. Bring to a boil, then reduce the heat to a simmer. Simmer, covered and stirring occasionally, until the meat is tender, about 1 hour. Taste and adjust for seasoning with salt and pepper. Serve immediately.

Round Steak and Okra Gumbo. *Prepared by chef Steven Goff, photograph courtesy of Peter Taylor.*

Okra Soup. *Prepared by chef Steven Goff, photograph courtesy of Peter Taylor.*

Okra Soup

by Chef Michael W. Twitty

Okra soup was raved about throughout the 1800s, so I'm excited to include this recipe from James Beard Foundation award-winning food historian and chef Michael Twitty. Twitty cares deeply about the origins of food and celebrates its heritage through his cooking and his writing.

Here is his introduction to the okra soup:

> *Here is a peppery, historically inspired recipe for Okra Soup. This version is based on recipes from the 19th century, especially those of Mary Randolph's* The Virginia Housewife *(1824) and Mrs. B. C. Howard's* Fifty Years in a Maryland Kitchen *(1881 edition). This simple DIY heirloom recipe has a few modern updates. The culinary trinity of hot pepper, tomato, and okra served with rice reinforce this soup's connection to similar dishes found from Senegal to Angola, and Philadelphia to Bahia.*

4 tablespoons butter

1 tablespoon lard or olive oil
(use olive oil to keep kosher)

1 small onion, diced and dusted
with flour

2 tablespoons finely chopped
flat-leaf parsley

1 clove garlic, minced

1 sprig fresh thyme

1 teaspoon salt

½ teaspoon kitchen pepper

½ teaspoon red pepper flakes

4 cups (960 ml) beef, chicken, or
vegetable broth

3 cups (750 ml) water

1 can (28 fl. oz. / 800 g) tomatoes
with juice, or 3½ cups (630 g)
peeled and diced fresh tomatoes

2 cups (200 g) fresh young okra,
cut into small, thin pieces, or
frozen okra pieces

2 cups (320 g) cooked rice,
kept hot or warm (optional)

In a Dutch oven, heat the butter and lard or olive oil until melted. Add the onion and finely chopped parsley and gently cook until the onion is translucent and soft. Add the garlic and cook for a minute more till fragrant. Add the thyme, salt, black pepper, and red pepper flakes and cook for another minute or so. Add the broth, water, and tomatoes and cook on a medium simmer for 30 minutes. Add the okra and cook for another 20 to 25 minutes, or until tender. Ladle into bowls over a ¼-cup (40 g) lump of warm rice each. Serve.

Note: To make this recipe kosher, use olive oil and vegetable broth.

> FOR THE KITCHEN PEPPER. Grind together 1 teaspoon coarsely ground black pepper, 1 teaspoon ground white pepper, 1 teaspoon red pepper flakes, 1 teaspoon ground mace, 1 teaspoon ground Ceylon cinnamon, 1 teaspoon ground nutmeg, 1 teaspoon ground allspice, and 1 teaspoon ground ginger.

Old-Time Okra Soup (from 1832)

by John Legare

This recipe was originally published in *The Southern Agriculturist* in 1832 and is almost certainly the written wisdom of enslaved black cooks. At the same time it represents a melding of cultures with the introduction of lima beans and corn and tomatoes, none of which are traditional African crops. The long cooking is quite different from many modern soup preparations; as Legare described, all the ingredients meld to become a delicious homogeneous mass. Okra Soup was loved throughout the 1800s, and perhaps it's time for a comeback.

I take one peck of okra pods, which must be very tender . . . cut them across into very thin slices, not exceeding ⅛ in. in thickness, but as much thinner as possible, as the operation is accelerated by their thinness. To this quantity of okra add about one third of a peck of tomatoes, which are first peeled and cut into pieces. This quantity can be either increased or diminished as may suit the taste of those for whom it is intended. A coarse piece of beef, (a shin is generally made use of) is placed into a digester [an early version of the pressure cooker] with about two and a half gallons of water and a very small quantity of salt. It is permitted to boil for a few moments, when the scum is taken off and the okra and tomatoes thrown in. These are all the ingredients that are absolutely necessary, and the soup made is remarkably fine. We however usually add some corn cut off from the tender roasting ears, (the grain from three ears will be enough for the above quantity.) We also add sometimes about a half pint of Lima or civie beans, both of these improve the soup, but not so much as to make them indispensables . . . The most material thing to be attended to is the boiling; and the excellence of the soup depends almost entirely on this being faithfully done; for if it be not enough, however well the ingredients may have been selected, the soup will be very inferior, and give but little idea of the delightful flavor it possesses when properly done . . . Should there be no digester, then an earthenware pot should be prepared, but on no account make use of an iron one as it would turn the wholesome soup perfectly black. The proper color being green, colored with the rich yellow of the tomatoes. The time which is usually occupied in boiling okra soup is five hours . . . By the time it is taken off, it will be reduced to about one half . . . I will state the criterion by which this is judged of—the meat separates entirely from the bone, being "done to rags." The whole appears as one homogenous mass, in which none of the ingredients are seen distinct; the object of this long cooking being thus to incorporate them. Its consistency should be about that of milk and porridge.

Old-Time Okra Soup.

CHAPTER 5

How to Eat Okra All Winter

I ate so much okra, I slid out of bed.

—Circa 1930s, author unknown

A complaint I hear all too often is that people don't like to grow okra because it's too productive. And that leads me to imagine myself sitting at a desk in some top-floor office with an impressive view of skyscrapers and sky. I'm wearing a suit, which is how you can tell I have a good imagination. There is a knock on the door, soft and hesitant.

"Come in," I say. The door opens.

"You wanted to see me," says Okra.

"Take a seat," I say.

"I finished that stack of papers," offers Okra.

I slam my palm on the table. Okra jumps.

"That's exactly why I called you in here," I growl.

Okra looks at me. Silent, fearful.

"Do I need to spell it out?" I ask.

Okra nods.

"You. Are. Too. Productive. Now get out, and stop overperforming."

I understand the foreboding that accompanies heading out to harvest okra with the knowledge that your fridge is already full of unprocessed pods; it's a sinking feeling of losing control. But it's not a good reason to avoid growing okra. If your okra production overtakes your okra consumption, as it's very able to do, there are several tactics you can employ. (*Note*: This is after you have given "gifts" to friends and family and started hiding baskets of okra in random unlocked cars.)

- Start eating/using the flowers. I explain the beauty of this solution in chapter 6, but basically, the flowers you eat can't produce pods.
- Leave some pods intact to mature on the plants. Then you can collect the pods and do fun things with the seeds, as I describe in chapter 8.
- Try one or more of the many ways to preserve okra so you'll never be without it through those long okra-less winter months. This chapter describes how to freeze, dehydrate, can, ferment, and pickle okra.

Freezing

Freezing produce is my least favorite storage method because of the fact that the end product has to be kept frozen. I suffer nightmares of the apocalypse where the grid goes down and my okra thaws and the ice cream melts and my family and I are forced to invite over all the neighbors and have an okra ice cream party. And everyone says, "I never knew okra could be so awesome." And finally I'm happy that okra is accepted and loved even though it took an apocalypse and a sugar high to realize it.

"I scream, you scream, we all scream for okra," says Okra.

Despite my nightmares, the freezer definitely has a place in a food preservation plan. Freezing food is quick and easy and, with many vegetables, the quality and the nutrition of the frozen food are quite high. Some instructions recommend first soaking the pods in a water-vinegar solution, but that type of treatment usually comes with the following type of note: "The acetic acid in the vinegar kills bacteria and helps to dissolve the wax, pesticide, and fertilizer residues."[1] I think I'll keep growing my own, or maybe I should start an organic okra farm . . .

"I'll call it OK RAnch," I say.

"No!" exclaim Okra *and* Belle.

If you are freezing okra you've grown yourself, you won't need to worry about wax, pesticide, and fertilizer residues on your pods. But if you don't have garden space to grow okra for processing, then check out your local farmers markets around the end of August. This is likely to be around the time that some farmers would be happy to ditch large quantities of okra at a good price. In addition, speaking to the farmer who grows your food is second best to growing it yourself, because it gives you the opportunity to ask questions. Small farmers don't need to be certified USDA Organic to be selling great produce. They may be uncertified but use organic methods; they may be certified Naturally Grown or biodynamic growers. Ask the questions!

Freezing okra pods is easy to do. The first step is to blanch the okra. Blanching is the process of scalding in boiling water for a set period of time.

Blanching basically halts vegetative matter in its metabolic tracks, stopping the enzyme action that leads to a loss of flavor, color, and texture. Blanching is time-sensitive: Under-blanching is worse than no blanching because it stimulates those enzymes you are trying to halt, and overblanching can cause a loss of vitamins and minerals. Fortunately the National Center for Home Food Preservation has researched blanching times for most vegetables. Ideal okra blanching times are 3 minutes for small pods and 4 minutes for large pods. One gallon (3.8 L) of water to 1 pound (453 g) of okra should be sufficient. Start timing from the moment the water returns to a boil after you've placed the okra in the pan.

I blanch a batch or two whenever I build up a surplus pile of okra. Immediately after blanching, abort the cooking process by dunking the okra into a bowl or tub of cold or iced water for about the same amount of time that you blanched the okra. Drain the cooled, blanched okra through a colander. You can freeze the pods whole or chop them into pieces first. When freezing okra for use as fried okra, go ahead and mix the sliced okra with cornmeal prior to freezing. A final trick is to spread slices or pods in a single layer on a baking sheet and flash-freeze them before placing them in a freezer bag or other container. Otherwise you'll end up with a solid mass of frozen okra (which if I'd ever been silly enough to do, I would tell you is really annoying).

Frozen okra makes a great addition to soups and gumbos (although I prefer using dried okra for this), but the way I most enjoy using frozen okra is grilling or roasting. I cut pods in half before blanching, and I freeze the cut pods in 1-pound (453 g) batches ready to be oiled, salted, and oven-roasted as a quick and delicious winter vegetable.

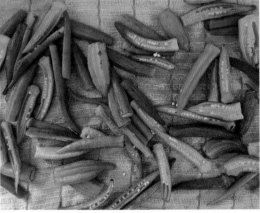

To freeze okra, start by blanching it in boiling water (I do this on an outside burner to avoid superheating my kitchen in summer). Freeze the okra in a single layer to avoid formation of one large frozen clump. Once the pods are frozen, you can transfer them to a more practical container.

Foraging for Okra in the Urban Landscape

As field research, I toured supermarkets around Asheville on the hunt for okra. I already knew that okra chips (packaged in Taiwan) are usually available at Trader Joe's. I don't go to Trader Joe's very often myself, but my officemate bribes me with okra chips to entice me to clean my desk, and that gives me a pretty good sense of their stocking schedule (my desk gets messy often). Whole Foods maintains a year-round supply of fresh okra. One time I bought some and the cashier had to look up the purchase code, saying, "I can never remember the code for okra because no one ever buys it."

"Ouch," says Okra.

"People are usually more polite in the South," I say.

Greenlife (a rebranded Whole Foods local to Asheville) serves sausage and okra gumbo from their hot bar. Earth Fare, a southeastern health food chain currently vacillating between being a Whole Foods wannabe and your friendly local health food store, carries no okra (with incredible mind-reading customer service, Earth Fare began stocking fresh okra about a week after I wrote the first draft of this chapter). Ingles, our local mid-range regular supermarket chain, always has a full shelf of frozen okra with pre-breaded and naked options. I have yet to find organically grown okra for sale in any supermarket, fresh or frozen.

Farmers markets abound in Asheville, and okra appears in season, with organic options available. There are also a couple of local picklers who preserve the taste of summer in vinegar and sell it throughout the region. Most of the supermarkets carry a pickled okra option, too, but I like local when I can find it.

I discovered a new way to eat frozen okra when I struck up a conversation with an exhibitor at the 2018 Georgia Organics Conference and Expo.

"I actually eat okra every single day," Denise Carroll told me, almost embarrassed.

Carroll went on to educate me about Trim Healthy Mama (THM) and its Okra Challenge. A THM eZine from 2016 encourages website visitors to "Take the 'Okra Challenge' and try to get this incredible veggie in several times a week." The top recommendation from the THM website for tackling the Okra Challenge is the Secret Big Boy smoothie: "Secret Big Boys are new takes on our original 'Big Boy Smoothie.' They are large and satisfying protein drinks that soothe digestion, moisturize your insides, and help shed stubborn pounds. The 'secret' comes from the fact that you would never guess all that creamy goodness contains a full cup of okra—unless somebody spills the beans. Don't spill the beans!"

"You just spilled the beans," says Okra.

"It's an okra *smoothie*!" I crow.

I swear this kind of thing should be on billboards. I prepared a Secret Big Boy for my unwitting guinea pigs, aka my family, without revealing the secret to them. I excitedly presented a tall glass of gloopy coffee-pumpkin smoothie to Belle and stepped back, waiting for a reaction.

"Does it have okra in it?" Belle asked.

"You've not even tasted it," I said.

Belle raised a single eyebrow, and I knew it was time to find a new guinea pig.

Dehydrating

An Okra Evaporator sounds like the evil invention of the AOA (Anti Okra Alliance)—a handheld ray gun that can be fired at okra to make it disappear in a poof of smoke, cackling optional. But actually it's a real invention, dating from the year 1900,[2] when okra was still popular and ray guns to vanquish vegetables were still secret technology. John Bradford of Springfield, Illinois (not related to Nat Bradford of the Bradford Family Okra), basically set up a giant dehydrator and an awesome marketing campaign for "Evaporated Okra." His advertisements appear in midwestern newspapers throughout the early 1900s.

Dehydrating food allows you to store it in a cool and dry location without any additional energy input during storage. At John Bradford's factory-scale operation, he dehydrated hundreds of pounds of okra on wire mesh in large kilns. I have a small five-shelved tabletop dehydrator, which works for my home-scale needs. There are lots of options on the market but I like mine because it has a timer and I can set the temperature. You can also dehydrate okra in your oven if it has a really low temperature setting and you can prop the door open.

Building a solar dehydrator is a priority item on my long to-do list. There are some excellent and relatively simple designs that utilize the sun's heat and the convection effect of rising hot air to dehydrate okra (or any other vegetable). I'm excited about solar dehydrators because using an electric dehydrator indoors in summer is twice stupid—first, it uses electricity to do what the sun can achieve for free, and second, it heats the house that air-conditioning costs to cool. Next year my solar dehydrator will make the whole process carbon- and cost-free.

Chef BJ Dennis simply lays okra pods on pieces of cardboard in the high summer heat for a day or two. "Dehydrating okra is simple," he told me. "Real simple." Dennis, whose given name is Benjamin Dennis IV, explored much of his personal heritage through his grandfather, Benjamin Dennis II. In his grandfather's time people would lay okra pods on the tin roofs of their houses to dry. "You don't see that anymore," Dennis said. "Everyone has freezers." While Dennis and I were having this phone conversation, he was cooking up some okra with foraged wild pokeweed and sweet potatoes. "Just for myself," he told me. "But it's something you wouldn't be surprised to find on one of my menus."

I asked Dennis if he thought there was much difference between frozen and dehydrated okra. He said that dried okra has a more intense flavor, but even though dehydrated okra regains some of its satisfying slipperiness when rehydrated into soups, it doesn't have the same okra texture that you can capture by freezing okra.

"My grandfather told me about a favorite wintertime stew," said Dennis. "It used dried okra, dried creek shrimp, and sun-dried tomatoes." But this was in a time before freezers were common, when dehydrating was a necessity for winter preservation.

I came across an old pamphlet on growing okra that described the Turkish tradition of threading okra pods on a string to hang for dehydrating: "A variety much used for drying is that known as petite gumbo or small okra. The pods of this variety are selected when only about one-half inch in

Emily and I do a test run stringing okra with a large plastic needle and some dental floss!

length and of uniform size. These are strung on a coarse fiber and hung to dry."[3] Emily and I found a large plastic needle and some dental floss and strung some okra to dry. The task was time consuming, but we gained speed as we practiced. This is one of those mindless tasks that is best done in community or while binge-watching Netflix. I've noticed that whole peppers dry faster when strung than when left on drying racks. The same was true of okra, and I think the small puncture of the skin by the needle is enough to help facilitate faster drying.

Dried okra is making somewhat of a comeback as a modern snack food (but not, sadly, as an ingredient in cooking). Freeze-dried okra pods are crunchy and slightly addictive. A bag of okra chips is really light—a couple of ounces at most—but it wasn't until I made my own that I realized how much okra is embodied in each bag. In my own experiments, approximately 2 pounds (907 g) of fresh okra yields about 4 ounces (113 g) of chips. That's quite the reduction through moisture loss! I've made my own whole-pod okra chips by seasoning the pods with a little oil, salt, and spices and then roasting them in the oven at 500°F (260°C) for 20 minutes and then 170°F (75°C) for about 2–3 hours (with the door propped open). When properly dried, the chips are a crunchy snack with lots of flavor that holds up well when you store them in a sealed jar.

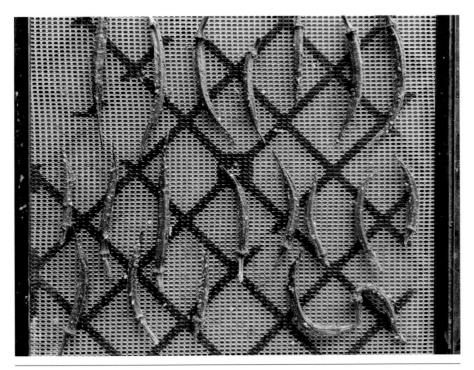

Dehydrated okra pods that have been oiled and seasoned are a super-tasty snack.

Dehydrated okra rings store well in a sealed jar for winter soups and stews. *Photograph courtesy of Peter Taylor.*

I've tried various methods of dehydrating okra. I like slicing the pods thin and crosswise—it takes more time to prepare the slices but less time to dehydrate. The tiny dried okra stars pack well into a jar, and I add them to soups through the winter. Dehydrating the pods whole takes longer (12–16 hours), so I tend to do this only when I'm making dehydrated okra snacks. I'll oil and season the pods in much the same way I'd make chips in the oven, sometimes with chili powder for spice, or rosemary and thyme so Emily will eat them. The difference is that I skip the super-hot oven and just let them dehydrate at around 135°F (57°C). The end product is a mixture of brittle crunchy pods and soft chewy ones (depending on the original size). They are surprisingly addictive. A good compromise between thin rings and whole pods is to cut the pods in half lengthwise. This dramatically reduces the cutting time and drying time, and there are plenty of recipes where lengthwise-sliced okra is preferred.

One traditional preparation of dried pods is to pound them into flour to add to various dishes as a flavoring and thickening agent. "The pounded dry okra has roots all the way back to West Africa," BJ Dennis told me. One report states that in Nigeria, okra pods are sun-dried for three days and then stored in baskets and clay pots. The dried okra is ground as needed, using a mortar and pestle.[4] The Gullah Geechee have maintained many of the West African culinary traditions, "inventing a form of Creole southern cooking," stated a report by the National Park Service on preserving the Gullah Geechee Corridor.[5] In the Sahel region of Africa, the pounded okra pod flour is used in the preparation of couscous, as it prevents the granules from sticking to one another.[6] And I've found that dehydrating and grinding overgrown pods into flour is a great way to make use of pods that are usually

Once fresh pods are dehydrated, they can be ground into a fine powder and used as a thickener, binder, and flavoring.

deemed inedible. I keep the pod flour in jars and add it to all sorts of things including veggie patties (for its sticking power), soups (for its thickening effect), and rice and couscous (for its flavor).

My research led me to another fascinating use of dried okra. Francis Morean is an ethnobotanist, traditional healer, author, and community historian. One of his main projects is documenting the history and food cultures of the small Caribbean island of Carriacou. Over the last 15 years, he has interviewed many islanders to capture some of these histories. Morean told me, "The island has a strong African presence, with very pronounced ancestral ceremonies and characteristics, which have allowed many of the islanders to be able to trace their roots to various 'nations' in West Africa."

Morean was quick to tell me that grassroots people of the Caribbean refer to okra as *ochroes*. In some Caribbean countries, young ochroes are a critical ingredient in a thick soup called callaloo. (*Callaloo* has multiple spellings and multiple meanings depending where you are in the Caribbean.) In Trinidad and Tobago, callaloo is made from ochroes and the leaves and stem of the taro plant. Morean said, "[Ochroes] must be young enough where they can become literally liquefied during preparation of the soup, without leaving any coarse fibers."

What follows is a brief look at some of the history around a callaloo that is specific to the island of Carriacou. "In Carriacou the term *callaloo* is used to describe a product which is quite distinct from other parts of the Southern Caribbean. It has a more pronounced traditional African culinary influence than in other parts of the region."

I've selected a few extracts from Morean's original interview transcripts, which retain the interviewees' vernacular. There are references to *cou cou*, a traditional African dish made from grated dry corn. *Benne* is a term for "sesame" and *groundnuts* refers to peanuts.

Former educator Sydney Cudjoe was 79 years old when Morean interviewed him. Cudjoe told Morean, "Benne is a Carriacou thing. I used to grow it. In the rainy season we used to plant a lot of ochroes. When we had plenty we dried some. We cut it up first and then dried it. In the dry season when you did not have fresh ochroes you grind the dried ochroes together with the dried groundnuts and the dried benne and you made a sauce. We called that sauce dried callaloo. We ate it with cou cou. It tasted very good."

Charles Solomon Clouden, a Rastafarian engaged in organic farming and herbal medicines, calls himself Ras Earth. He was 53 years old when Morean interviewed him. Ras Earth said, "Me parents used to plant plenty benne. Me parents also had plenty ochro. They used to cut up the ochro and put it to dry. When it dry you store it away. When you come to cook it now you pound it in a mata and pestle until it came to a powder then we sift it in a piece of veil. We had no strainers in those days. Then we pound the benne separate. Then we pound some groundnut and you put all that together with the benne and the ochro and put it to boil. You could put a piece of any corn fish in that and you made a gravy. You eat that with your cou cou. That was the healthiest food that I knew."

I made an approximation of this powder and first used it as a dry seasoning on rice. It was deeply flavored and I could imagine it enhancing any number of dishes. I mixed some with water to make a kind of sauce, which thickened quickly into a paste; at that stage it resembled a souped-up pad Thai peanut sauce, but adding more water turned it more soupy. Adding fish or chicken to the sauce at that stage would turn it into a complete and tasty meal.

The Carriacou are a long-lived people, and Morean pondered whether their diet, rich in ochroes and taro, could be the source of their good health. His research is fascinating and ongoing.

I prepared a dried version of Carriacou callaloo with ground ochroes, ground parched sesame, and peanuts, served over rice. *Photograph courtesy of Peter Taylor.*

33749. ABELMOSCHUS ESCULENTUS (L.) Moench. Okra

(*Hibiscus esculentus L.*)

From Avery Island, La. Presented by Mr. E. A. McIlhenny. Received May 31, 1912.

These seeds are from a species of okra a friend of ours sent us from Egypt six or seven years ago. By careful selection we have produced a variety of okra which is unexcelled for table purposes. It is an early bearer and has a thicker flesh and is more tender than any of the commercial okra which we have tried. (*McIlhenny*)[7]

I reached out to the McIlhenny Company, which is still family-owned, and spoke with their historian and curator Dr. Shane K. Bernard. "We [the company] grew and canned okra in the early 20th century in a short-lived side business called the McIlhenny Canning and Manufacturing Company," he told me.

Dr. Bernard sent me a photo of an original can of okra (opened) and dated it around 1905, which would be before or around the time that E. A. McIlhenny started developing his improved Egyptian okra variety. I wanted to know if that okra variety still existed, or perhaps was even used today in the same way that the Tabasco pepper has been preserved. Dr. Bernard dug up an archived telegram from the company records, dated December 18, 1917. It stated that the only variety grown by the McIlhenny Company was White Velvet, which doesn't bode well for the continued existence of the Egyptian variety. It's likely another lost seed and another unsolvable mystery.

◉ ◉ ◉

Another large and well-known company in the world of canning also engaged in breeding work: Campbell Soup Company. A 1910 issue of the *Saturday Evening Post* contains no fewer than six advertisements for Campbell's Condensed Soup, including okra-tomato and chicken-gumbo-okra, at 10 cents a can (and the proclamation that it's as easy as making a cup of tea). These ads are among the early signs of our food industry prioritizing cost and convenience. I contacted the company in the hope of finding a Campbell's version of Dr. Bernard, but it was not to be. I did speak to a company representative. The first conversation concerned clarifying questions about my request.

"Campbell's okra varieties, you say?"

"Four varieties actually—most of them aren't very well known, but Emerald is still known and grown today," I told the representative. "Seed companies credit Campbell's as the breeder of Emerald okra all the time."

"Interesting," he said. I think his name was Brian.

A variety called Campbell's Long Green was developed in 1940 (parentage: selection from Perkins Mammoth). In 1945 Campbell's released a variety called Evergreen (parentage: Clemson Spineless, Lady Finger) and another called Perkins Spineless (parentage: Campbell's Long Green, Clemson Spineless). In 1950 the company released Emerald (parentage: Campbell's Long Green, Clemson Spineless, Louisiana Green Velvet, Cow Horn).

Brian called back over a month later.

"I have nothing to tell you," he said.

"Nothing?"

"Nope, sorry."

"You mean to tell me that your company bred and released okra varieties, one of which is still grown and sold across the country with your name attached, and you can't tell me anything about the breeding program?"

"That's correct," said Brian.

My budding investigative journalism career came to an abrupt halt.

"Google?" says Okra.

"Google," I agree.

Google turned out to be almost as uninformative as Brian. I did learn about Campbell's Agricultural Research Center. The center was established in 1948 and originally focused on breeding tomatoes, peas, carrots, and potatoes, but later switched to tomatoes and peppers. No mention of okra. In 2012 the Campbell Soup Company sold its seed-breeding operation to HM Clause, a global seed company. I contacted HM Clause and received a quick reply stating they had no records of Campbell's breeding okra. Campbell's still sells a chicken gumbo soup, and okra is listed as an ingredient. However, my personal suggestion is that you buy a packet of Emerald okra seeds, grow your own okra, then make and can your own gumbo to enjoy all winter!

Pickling and Fermenting

"The pickle plate is making a comeback," chef Vivian Howard wrote in *Deep Run Roots*. She was referring to a Crock-Pot full of fermented summer vegetables that would be served on a plate when guests came over. Her pickle plate recipe contains whole okra, 2-inch (5 cm) chunks of corn on the cob, hot peppers, and garlic with pepper and salt, and it tastes delicious. Howard used the term *pickle plate* to refer to a plate of fermented vegetables, which is totally correct, even though today most people think of pickling and fermenting as two separate things. Today most items referred to as pickles are pickled in acetic acid (vinegar), but pickling in lactic acid is an age-old method of food preservation that is commonly called fermenting. One big difference is that fermentation creates a live, active culture with the natural lactic acid present in all vegetables, whereas vinegar pickling creates a sterile environment. Both methods are great ways to preserve and eat okra.

Bringing up the subject of pickling okra in a public place is almost as dangerous as talking about fried okra. It seems as though everyone wants to share their grandmother's pickling spice recipe that has been handed down through the family. In my experience I can throw in whatever I have in the cupboard (peppercorns, mustard seeds, bay leaves, dried chili peppers . . .), and my okra pickles turn out pretty tasty. One ingredient does stand out as essential for optimal results: turmeric. I've noticed that turmeric shows up on the label of the best store-bought pickles as well as in the ingredients list of good pickle recipes. Sean Brock's cookbook *Heritage* includes a recipe for Pickled Okra he learned from celebrity chef Robert Carter and described as "one of the best pickled okra recipes I have ever tasted." And yes, it contains turmeric, as well as garlic and hot peppers, mustard seeds and salt. One top tip from Sean Brock is to gently slit the pod just under the stem cap. This will allow the pods to fill with vinegary goodness without releasing slime. (See "Pickled Okra" on page 99 for the recipe.)

One thing I love about vinegar pickling is that you can seal the jars in a hot-water bath and then store the pickles for a long time with no need for refrigeration (the storage area should be cool and dark). Store-bought pickles obviously have a use-by date, and home pickles have a recommended one to two years of shelf life. I suspect, though, that pickles have the potential to survive the apocalypse and some decades beyond. As the climate continues changing and sea levels rise, perhaps floating jars of pickled okra will bob around on the high seas and offer hope to marooned islanders clinging to the highlands of old. I haven't been able to test the longevity of my pickles because they don't last long enough! In fact just last night as I pondered pickled okra, I opened my last jar from last season's harvest. (It's April as I write this.) My store of dehydrated okra will have to tide me over until fresh okra is ready again in the summer, but pickled okra is what comes closest to capturing the taste of summer. I think the addition of turmeric, which offers a golden sheen to the pickled pods, triggers a memory of the summer sun as much as a depth of flavor. Perhaps I'll pickle some okra with yellow food coloring and see if it induces the same feeling of a summer captured and preserved.

"Hell N'okra!" says Okra.

All the ingredients for a big batch of okra pickles have been collected and are ready to process.

Sandor Katz had this to say about okra in his incredible book *The Art of Fermentation*:

> *If you enjoy okra, try fermenting some. I usually use okra whole, mixing them with shredded vegetables. That way their sliminess remains mostly enclosed within them, so the people (like me) who enjoy that can, while others can simply avoid the okra. If you chop the okra with other vegetables, the whole batch can take on okra's slime (yum).*

I like a person who appreciates their okra slime and reached out to Sandor Katz to see what more he had to offer on fermenting okra. He told me he likes to ferment okra with green beans and shared his procedure (see

This fermenting vessel packed full of okra and spices just needs topping off with brine. Fermenting vessels like these come with stones to keep the okra submerged during fermentation.

"Fermented Okra," page 96). Fermenting can be a very personal endeavor, and I encourage you to play and experiment with your ferments. Vegetables such as shredded cabbage can produce enough moisture once salted that they'll ferment in their own juices, but whole okra pods need to be submerged in a salt brine to begin the fermenting process. The speed of the fermentation depends on the temperature and the quantity of salt (more salt slows it down; more heat speeds it up). But the readiness of a fermentation is also subjective. The pods will continue to get softer and then mushier the longer they ferment, but the sourness and the flavors will also continue to develop. I once had a jarful that I called 365-Day Okra. I had fermented some okra and forgot about one jar. I found it in the basement a year later. I challenge you to come up with something slimier than year-old fermented okra—but amazingly, all the flavors of okra, hot peppers, garlic, and spices had melded into a delectable concoction. I swear if I'd had oyster shells on hand I could have put a spoonful of okra gloop in a shell and sold faux-oyster okra for a dollar a pop. If oyster bars want a vegan option, this is it.

I asked Katz about another reference to okra in *The Art of Fermentation*. He told of a woman from Texas who shared a story about fermenting okra that had gone a little woody: "Even woody, tough okra that would not have been good fried or in gumbo was just heavenly when fermented in brine for a couple of days." Since the rapid development of pod woodiness is a common complaint from okra growers, the possibility of rescuing woody pods through fermentation was exciting. Sadly, I've not been able to replicate her heavenly experience, and Katz had the following comment: "Generally I find the tough fibrous ones stay tough when you ferment them, and you just end up chewing them and sucking out all the delicious flavor and seeds and non-fibers, then spitting out the fibers." My guess is the pods that the Texan was describing were larger than those she usually ate, but not yet truly woody.

◉ ◉ ◉

Chef Steven Goff, who describes himself as a meat and pickle man, has honed his skills to support a belief that there should be no waste in the kitchen, a belief informed to some extent by growing up poor and living dwelling-free at the beginning of his career. In our early communications he revealed his love for okra. "Definitely one of my top five vegetables," he said. "Last year I made okra kimchi."

Goff is the executive chef and partner of Aux Bar in downtown Asheville, where the menu specializes in regional and seasonal ingredients from the Appalachian South. I was lucky enough to spend a morning in the kitchen with Goff and help in the creation of a fresh batch of okra kimchi.

Chef Steven Goff and I make a batch of okra kimchi at Aux Bar in Asheville. We first roll the pods over coarse salt, then mix them with a premade chi sauce.

Inspired by his experiences with the Japanese technique for making *nuka-zuke*—which uses rice bran (*nuka*)—Goff rolled the okra pods over a layer of coarse grain salt. This allowed the salt to penetrate the skin and begin the fermentation process without releasing the slime. As the pile of salted okra grew, it visibly sweated as the salt drew moisture out of the pods. We were rolling red okra in salt, which stained both the salt and our hands a beautiful purple. Pods of all shapes and sizes went into the ferment, stems and all, no waste! "Kimchi is a great kitchen trash can," said Steve. "I collect all sorts of vegetable scraps and ferment them."

We crushed and shoved the okra into jars without ceremony, adding layers of chi paste that filled the gaps. (See "Okra Kimchi" on page 100 for the recipe.) Like Sandor Katz, and most serious fermenters I know, Goff embraced a casual bit-of-this, bit-of-that style. He threw in some liquid from another ferment to act as starter culture. In part I'm sure Goff's casual approach to creating kimchi is a product of years of experience, but it's also an awesome element of fermenting. You get to go a little wild in the kitchen and see what happens! The Okra Kimchi ferment smelled delicious, but I had to wait a few weeks before returning to get the full taste experience.

It was worth it: a tangy, fruity, little-bit-spicy, still-crunchy okra delight. The red pods held their color, and everything remained glazed in the thick kimchi sauce. I enjoy okra in all shapes and forms, but this is one recipe that seared itself into my mouth memory. Every time I think about it, I begin to drool. I swallow the excess saliva, but if I were a dog, it'd be messy.

One last element of the Okra Kimchi is from an idea inspired by Jamie Swofford, a chef-turned-farmer who focuses on flavor. Swofford explained how he dehydrates his ferments. He creates powdered kimchi and uses it as a seasoning that carries the concentrated flavor of the ferment: "Sprinkle a little on fresh cucumber and you get all the crunchy texture of a fresh cucumber and all the flavor of a pickle!" Knowing how well okra dehydrates, and how tasty dried, ground okra pods are, I had to try making the Okra Kimchi spice.

Chef Steven Goff told me to dehydrate the kimchi at 115°F (45°C) or less; that way the powder can actually be used as a starter culture for other ferments, giving it one more useful application in the kitchen. As I expected, the powder turned out to be incredible. Such a magnificent blend of flavors could never fail. I'm definitely adding dehydrated ferments to my arsenal of kitchen preservation, and it's fitting that Okra Kimchi was my maiden voyage!

Fermented Okra

by Sandor Katz

I really enjoy fermenting food because of the freedom it allows. You can pretty much submerge any vegetable or spice mix in a salt brine and create something tasty. Sandor Katz, author of *The Art of Fermentation*, is my fermenting hero, and to discover he loves slimy okra was a special bonus. This recipe works in a 1-quart jar, but you can scale up and ferment in a larger jar or a ceramic crock. The length of fermentation is subjective and dependent on temperature, but anywhere from 3 days to 2 weeks is normal. You can substitute other seasonings for the dill, garlic, or peppercorns if desired.

1 pound (453 g) small tender okra
A few fresh chili peppers
  (optional)
2 tablespoons any form of dill
  (fresh or dried leaf or seeds,
  or a flowering head)
1–2 heads garlic
1 pinch whole black peppercorns
1½ tablespoons sea salt

Trim away any damaged or bruised spots on the pods. Clean the vessel, then place the seasonings at the bottom. Pack the whole pods into the vessel tightly to ensure they will remain submerged under the brine. Feel free to incorporate green beans, small pickling cucumbers, sweet peppers, green tomatoes, or other summer vegetables as desired.

Dissolve the sea salt in 2 cups (500 ml) dechlorinated water to create a brine solution. Stir until the salt is thoroughly dissolved. Add the brine to the vessel. If the brine doesn't cover the vegetables, add more brine mixed at the same ratio of ¾ tablespoon salt to 1 cup (250 ml) water. If the okra are floating at the surface, an easy solution is to cut the top of a plastic food container a little bigger than the mouth of the jar, squeeze it through the mouth of the jar, and position it so that it holds the okra submerged. If you're using a crock, use a plate to weigh down the okra and cover it with a cloth to keep out dust and flies. With a jar, use the lid to seal loosely.

Leave the okra to ferment 3 or 4 days, then taste every day or two. Sourness will develop over time; how fast depends primarily upon temperature. If any white surface scum appears, skim it off, but don't worry if you can't get it all. Enjoy the okra as they continue to ferment. Continue to check them regularly. If they start to soften, or if you don't want them to become any sourer, move them to the fridge.

Fermented Okra. *Photograph courtesy of Peter Taylor.*

Pickled Okra. *Photograph courtesy of Peter Taylor.*

Pickled Okra

by Sean Brock

MAKES 5 QUART JARS

Pickled may well be one of my favorite ways to eat okra, which is surprising given that I'm not usually a pickle fan. Pickled Okra is crunchy and tangy and spicy, and just thinking about it makes me want to run for my basement and crack open a jar of summer, captured in an okra pod. Chef Sean Brock's recipe has never failed me, and while his book *Heritage* has multiple okra recipes, this one is truly outstanding.

He wrote: "Here's your chance to try one of the best pickled okra recipes I have ever tasted. It's one I learned when I was an extern at Peninsula Grill under chef Robert Carter, one of my mentors, and I've made this pickled okra every year since."

5 pounds (2¼ kg) medium okra, washed

7½ cups (2 L) cider vinegar

3 cups (750 ml) water

7½ jalapeño peppers, thinly sliced into rounds, seeds included

7½ cloves garlic, thinly sliced

1½ cups (270 g) kosher salt

6 tablespoons sugar

1½ tablespoons turmeric

1½ tablespoons yellow mustard seeds

Sterilize five quart canning jars along with the rings and lids. Make a small slit at the base of each okra pod so that the pickling liquid can enter. Pack the okra tightly into the jars.

Combine the vinegar, water, jalapeño peppers, garlic, salt, sugar, turmeric, and mustard seeds in a large stainless steel pot and bring to a boil over high heat, stirring to dissolve the salt and sugar. Ladle the mixture over the okra, leaving a ½-inch (1.3 cm) headspace. Wipe the rims and threads clean. Put the lids and rings on the jars and finger-tighten the rings. Process the jars in a boiling-water bath for 15 minutes, adjusting for altitude.

It is important that jars seal properly and a vacuum forms. If any jars did not seal, you must store the okra in the refrigerator; allow them to cure for 1 week before eating. Properly sealed jars will keep in a cool, dark place for up to 6 months; refrigerate after opening.

Note: This recipe also works as a quick pickle. Halve the recipe, and skip the boiling-water bath processing. Instead, store the jars in the refrigerator. The okra will be ready in about 1 week; it will keep for up to 3 weeks after opening.

Okra Kimchi

by Chef Steven Goff

MAKES 1 QUART JAR

Okra Kimchi was not on my list of must-have recipes when I began writing this book, but stumbling upon chef Steven Goff and his love of okra and anything fermented was a chance encounter I'm truly grateful for. Not only is his Okra Kimchi one of the most delicious and surprising things I have ever tasted, but Goff invited me to his restaurant, Aux Bar, to experience making kimchi. Subsequently, he spent an entire day helping prepare many of the dishes you see beautifully photographed in this book.

½ cup (75 g) dried peppers
  (I use arboles)
1 cup (250 ml) water
1 cup (250 ml) canola oil
3 onions, julienned
2 leeks, sliced
1 cup (140 g) crushed garlic cloves
½ cup (50 g) chopped ginger,
  not peeled
1 cup (120 g) bread flour
1½ cups (375 ml) cider vinegar
½ cup (110 g) brown sugar
1 pound (453 g) whole okra pods

CHI PREPARATION

Plump the dried peppers by soaking them in the water. Heat the oil in a deep pan on medium-high. Add the peppers, onions, leeks, garlic, and ginger once the oil begins smoking. Continue to sauté the vegetables until translucent. Add the flour, vinegar, and sugar and cook for a further 3–5 minutes.

Purée with an immersion blender while the mixture is still hot.

POD PREPARATION

Roll the okra pods over a layer of coarse salt, sprinkled on a table or countertop. The aim is to puncture the pods with the coarse salt. Roll each pod individually and pile them all in a bowl. Let the okra and salt sit and sweat for 1–2 hours.

Slather the okra with the chi paste and then pack the mixture tightly into the jar. Cover the jar with plastic wrap and push out any remaining air. If there are any air gaps at the top of the jar, you can push the plastic down and fill with water to remove them. Cap the jar and leave at room temperature for at least a week. Burp the jar frequently and refrigerate when the okra is sour enough to suit your tastes.

Any remaining chi can be used in other kimchi projects or as a sauce.

Okra Kimchi. *Prepared by chef Steven Goff, photograph courtesy of Peter Taylor.*

Mayan Okra. *Photograph courtesy of Peter Taylor.*

CHAPTER 6

Take the Okra Flower Pledge

Okra not only has an enticing flower, but it's a seductive vegetable as well.

—Virginia Willis, *Okra*

I am often surprised to learn that even the most ardent okra supporters have never tasted an okra flower. So before you read this chapter, you must first take the Okra Flower Pledge. Hand on heart, repeat after me: "I solemnly pledge, upon my next immediate proximity to a flowering okra plant, laws of the land and common courtesy notwithstanding, to eat an okra flower."

The okra flower can be alluring and intimidating, like the Siren's Song. Focus too long on the voluptuous curves of the pastel creamy yellow flowers, opened trumpet-like to the sky, and you may fall victim to their beauty and fail to make good on your pledge. The okra flower is perfect and poetic, and has been described as follows: "Flowers open at dawn and are ebracteate, pedicellate, pentamerous, actinomorphic, hermaphrodite, complete, and hypogynous."[1] Or, for those of us who don't have a PhD in botany, flowers open at dawn and are unadorned by leaves or leaf-like structures; they form on a pedunculated stem, and each flower consists of five sections with radial symmetry. They have both male and female reproductive organs as well as a full accoutrement of petals and sepals, and the male reproductive parts are situated below the female. And yet each flower opens for only a day, to be pollinated and die. Job done, as we say in England.

The fact that a species is able to self-pollinate doesn't necessarily mean that it's particularly good at it. However, in the case of okra, one study showed 100 percent pollination in flowers that had been protected by special bags to deny insects access.[2]

These front and side views of okra flowers show off the beautiful trumpet-like shape.

"I'm very independent," says Okra.

Still, those flowers are big, showy, and beautiful, and they certainly attract their fair share of insect attention, unneeded or otherwise. Even though okra flowers are self-pollinating, many winged insects visit them. I've seen a range of bees and wasps zipping in and out of the flowers on the okra I have grown.

"Who doesn't like to be loved?" asks Okra.

"If only bees wrote the food columns," I say.

In this way okra is hedging its bets, happy and capable of self-pollinating its own flowers, but also encouraging the distribution of pollen among flowers via insects. A further reason for insects is the quality of pollination. Researchers in West Africa assessed quality by collecting data on the quantity of seed set within pods (as opposed to simply counting the percentage of pollinated flowers that formed pods). They found that pods with the highest quantity of well-formed seeds formed from insect-pollinated flowers, second highest from hand-pollinated flowers, and a significantly lower rate of seed set from bagged self-pollinated flowers.[3] In Jordan a study found the same results when they looked at insect pollination versus self-pollination in eight okra genotypes.[4] This data suggests that pollinators may play a more important role in okra production than previously assumed. Given the alarming declines of insect populations over recent decades, and the clear link between pollinators and food production for many vegetables,

I wonder how much okra production would be affected with limited insect pollination. I've observed fully grown pods that contain very few seeds, but I've also seen pods self-abort with no obvious cause.

Bumblebees and honeybees can pollinate okra, but there is also one special insect fan of the okra flower: *Ptilothrix bombiformis*, aka the okra bee. Dr. Nancy Adamson, a pollinator conservation specialist for the Xerces Society, turned me on to the presence of this hairy-legged, ground-nesting solitary bee. It's also known by a few other common names—the rose mallow bee, hibiscus bee, and eastern digger bee. Although okra is not a North American native, the okra bee is native to eastern North America. And beyond that, it is oligolectic, which means that it seeks out particular sources of pollen, often from only a single genus.[5] Before okra came to be grown in North America, this bee evolved in company with rose mallow and other native species, but once okra arrived *Ptilothrix* was ready to embrace it as a food source as well.

As I started my amateur entomology quest to find the okra bee, Adamson gave me good advice: If I found a bee that was not a bumblebee or a honeybee in an okra flower, there was a good chance it was an okra bee. With that in mind, I vowed to capture one of these okra allies on camera. I often worked my okra rows in the predawn hours, using a headlamp to harvest before it got unbearably hot, when all was quiet and still. The roosters would always crow first, preempting dawn, eerie on those early misty mornings. But as the sky lightened, the insects also woke. The okra flowers would barely unfurl before insects began buzzing inside them. Bumblebees and honeybees flowed around the okra patch, enjoying the morning sun and luxuriating in the flowers, but the okra bees would zip and zap with camera-blur speed. It's as if, linked as they were to okra, they alone knew that these flowers would already be dying in a few hours and had to maximize their pollen-gathering potential. "I'll sleep when I'm dead," they yelled, but even that came out as *zzzppppp*. After one frustrating morning trying to photograph the okra bee, but succeeding only in filling my camera with out-of-focus black blobs and streaks, I sat in my truck drinking cold coffee. Then I noticed a dead bee clinging to my shoulder. The poor little thing must have zipped and zapped itself to death. I couldn't help wonder why it had chosen my dark gray hoodie as its final resting place. Perhaps in a life

Meet *Ptilothrix bombiformis*, aka the okra bee. This is the poor bee that died on my hoodie, gracefully allowing itself to be photographed.

Here is *Ptilothrix bombiformis* in action, collecting pollen in an okra flower. *Photograph courtesy of Nancy Lee Adamson.*

filled with flowers, gray is where peace is found. Sad as I was for the end of the insect's life, it offered me an opportunity to marvel at its large black eyes, hairy hind legs, and beautiful laced wings: a perfect specimen of *Ptilothrix bombiformis.*

Eating the Flower

An English Cadbury's Cream Egg commercial I remember from childhood featured people eating their eggs in lots of creative ways: the gobbler, the nibbler, the licker—you get the idea. The tagline was, "How do you eat yours?" The same question may be asked of the okra flower eater. I must profess that I like to eat the flower whole, biting it off just above the stem, but you may prefer to nibble the petals like a rabbit until you are left with just the stem and the large central reproductive organ with the red stigma at its tip. Alone, without its exuberant collar of petals, this staminal column loses some of its authority. You may pull off and consume each petal individually, chanting aloud, "I love you, I love you not, I love you, I love you not, I love you." It's no coincidence that you'll always end up in love. It's the pentamerous nature of the flower.

I'll often eat a few flowers in the field as a tasty snack. *Photograph courtesy of Belle Crawford.*

Another approach is to eat the blossom from the stem end first. This strategy means you don't have to come face-to-face with the protruding reproductive parts and allows you to dangle the flower from your lips, cigar-like, before you munch it down. This is how I imagine a cow would choose to eat okra flowers if unobserved and graced with opposable thumbs.

I understand the novice's intimidation. The staminal column is covered in pollen-bearing stamens and wraps the delicate style linking the ovary (okra-pod-to-be) and the red stigma. Dr. Hans R. Dhingra works in the Department of Botany and Plant Physiology at the CCS Haryana Agricultural University in India, and he described some of okra's reproductive biology: "All floral parts except gynoecium are hairy . . . The inner extension of the petals, which is scalelike . . . The pollen grains are large, spherical, bicelled, and spiny with many pores . . . Stigmas are deep red or dark purple."[6] I suggest eating first and microscopic examination second.

Okra flowers are tasty and good for you. Flowers in general are a highly underutilized nutrient source. While edible flowers have been eaten for centuries, recent studies have proven their high mineral levels and strong antioxidant properties.[7] I include edible flowers in my diet for just one more notch of diversity in a modern food system that revolves around corn, soy, and wheat. Okra's cousin aibika, *Abelmoschus manihot*, has received

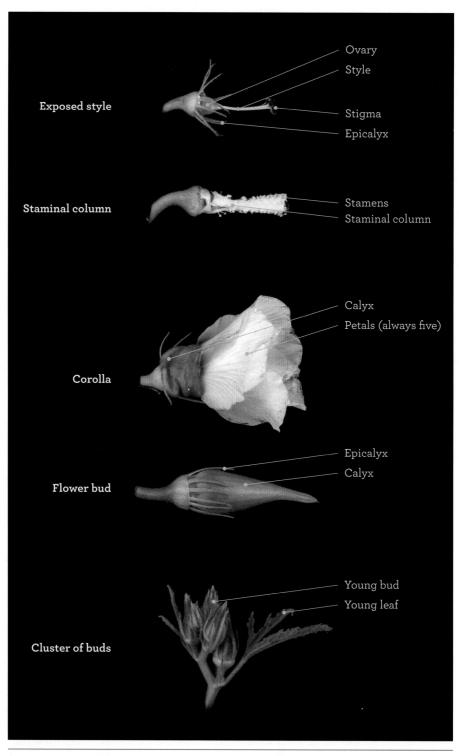

Exposed style
- Ovary
- Style
- Stigma
- Epicalyx

Staminal column
- Stamens
- Staminal column

Corolla
- Calyx
- Petals (always five)

Flower bud
- Epicalyx
- Calyx

Cluster of buds
- Young bud
- Young leaf

Here you can see all the parts of the okra flower identified with botanical precision. But feel free to just eat the flower!

Leaving No Stigma Untrimmed

The thought of saffron inspired me to experiment with okra stigmas. Saffron, one of the most prized spices in the world, is made of the stigmatic threads of the *Crocus sativus* flower. It takes 750,000 crocus flowers to yield enough stigmas (harvested by hand) to equal 1 kilogram (2.2 pounds) of dried saffron spice. For my experiment, I snipped approximately 100 okra stigmas from the end of the staminal columns and dried them to make a saffron substitute. Traditionally a pinch of saffron is ground into a powder and added to a pot of rice along with a pinch of unground threads. Okra stigmas are not threads, so I ground everything into a powder. My hope was for a sorrel-esque taste, a little like ground sumac seasoning, that would color my rice red. I ended up with a bland gray powder. Sad to say it, but displacement of the saffron industry is not an exciting example of a groundbreaking use for okra.

"Setting me up to fail," says Okra.

"I think it was Woody Allen who said, 'If you're not failing every now and then, it's a sign you're not doing anything very innovative,'" I say.

some attention for its medicinal flower, with multiple studies showings its anti-inflammatory, antibacterial, and anticoagulant effects (it also has edible leaves, and I cover that in chapter 7).[8] Other studies of the phyto-chemical properties of *A. manihot* flowers indicated that flavonoids separated from the flowers possessed various biological activities, including anti-inflammatory, antibacterial, antioxidant, and protective effects on the renal cellular membrane.[9] While similar studies would have to be conducted on okra, it seems highly possible that such a closely related flower would have similar properties.

As part of a joint promotion between Sow True Seed and Newman's Restaurant in Saluda, North Carolina, I was invited to an evening feast. It was a true expression of farm-to-table, where a majority of the food cooked had traveled less than 100 feet on its way from the garden to the kitchen to the table. As with many terms, one has to be wary of greenwashing by farm-to-table establishments. Technically any food served at a table can be described as farm-to-table; there are no laws that govern the use of this phrase. Nothing is written that defines what type of farm qualifies, or where the food went between the farm and the table. McDonald's could probably employ this terminology with a subtle revision: farm-to-car. When reading *farm-to-table* we rely on the integrity of the restaurant or food truck, and our own investigative powers; we rely on our ability to ask questions. Sadly,

of dried flower matter (probably around 30 flowers) before topping off with the vinegar. The liquid instantly started pulling out swirls of pink from the flowers. One quick stir turned the vinegar a deep pink. Within 24 hours it was deep red, and I knew this would be a stunning salad dressing vinegar.

I usually leave my vinegar extractions for about 4 weeks before straining out the vegetal matter and storing the liquid. After 4 weeks the okra flower vinegar had taken on some of the viscosity of okra mucilage in a way the vodka did not. I theorize that it's because I used dried flowers instead of fresh and thus the ratio of okra tissue to liquid was higher in the extract than in the vodka. Some herbalists don't like using fresh product in alcohol and vinegar tinctures, because the moisture content can dilute the vinegar/alcohol and compromise its preservative affect.

I made a salad dressing with okra flower vinegar, roasted okra seed sea salt, and okra seed oil and used it on Raw Okra Salad (see the recipe in chapter 2). I also used the vinegar to pickle some immature okra seeds. The color of the vinegar cut into the pale white-brown seeds and produced a vibrant garnish. They turned out looking like little pink fish eggs! Based on my research into *A. manihot* flowers and the rich colors I extracted from okra blossoms, I suspect these culinary tinctures include many of the beneficial and medicinal components of the flowers.

I didn't set out to create an okra flower line of drinks, but the flowers have proved themselves wonderful ingredients for that application. It's a

To make a vodka infusion, I stuffed fresh flowers (but dried is fine) into a container and covered them with vodka. The jar should remain sealed for 4–6 weeks; then the flowers can be strained out and composted, leaving you with a delicious okra flower vodka.

perfect way to capture their essence. By now I hope you're catching on that I approach everything with open-minded optimism and follow all paths with wide-eyed enthusiasm. It's a pretty fun approach to life.

"I'll drink to that," says Okra.

"Cheers!"

Immature okra seeds pickled in my red okra flower vinegar make a great garnish. *Photograph courtesy of Peter Taylor.*

To make okra flower vinegar, combine dried flowers with white vinegar. The pink color develops almost instantly; 4 weeks later, after you've strained out the flowers, the finished vinegar is rich red.

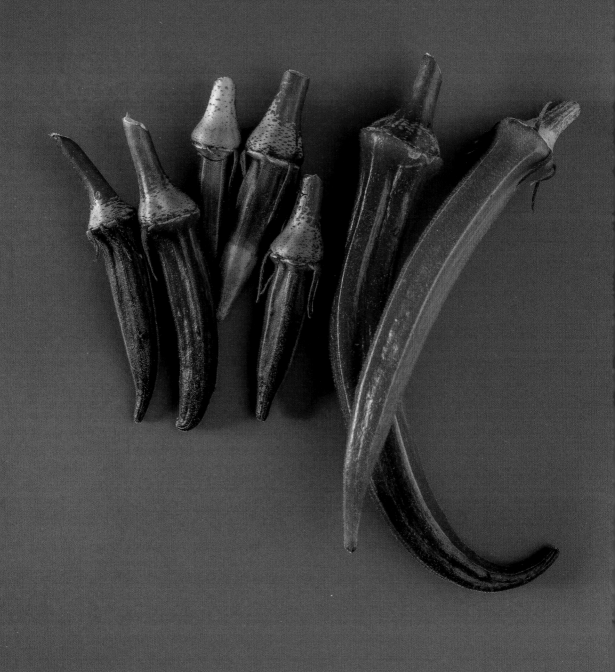

Sea Island Okra (Ethiopian Red). *Photograph courtesy of Peter Taylor.*

CHAPTER 7

Eat Your Greens

The plant that seems to hold the wealth of Midas within its branches.

—Vicksburg (MS) Evening Post, 1907[1]

I 'm known for asking people, "Did you know you can eat that?" One time, while I lamented on all the things that are edible but not eaten, someone commented, "Just because you *can* eat it, doesn't mean you *should*."

"Touché," says Okra.

"Whose side are you on?" I ask.

In the case of okra leaves, I would argue that you can and you should eat them. According to the 1977 classic *Vegetables for the Hot, Humid Tropics*, "The young leaves [of okra] are sometimes used as a fresh vegetable. Indeed, they are not only appetizing but also have a higher protein content than the pods. The use of leaves is especially recommended for vigorous, much-branched varieties from which harvests of leaves and pods can be taken."[2] Although when I first began researching the uses of okra leaves, two of the few stories I found involved the criminal underworld . . .

In October 2014 the *Washington Post* reported, "Heavily armed drug cops raid retiree's garden, seize okra plants." The story goes that a helicopter crew working for the Governor's Task Force for Drug Suppression were flying around suburban Georgia and spotted a suspicious crop. Based on that intel a heavily armed K-9 unit was dispatched to raid the property of Mr. Dwayne Perry and seize any illegal plant growth. Sadly, the illegal plant growth turned out to be an okra patch. The Georgia officers ended up apologizing, but still took some okra leaf samples for analysis. Patrol Captain Kermit Stokes commented that the plants did have characteristics similar to marijuana. The *Washington Post* retorted, "Indeed! Like cannabis, okra is green and it has leaves."

Coconut Cream Okra Leaf with Tilapia

by Chris Smith

SERVES 4

There are very few recipes that use okra leaves, and most that do exist simply call for adding leaves as one ingredient in a soup. However, okra has a close cousin, aibika (*Abelmoschus manihot*), whose leaves are regularly used in cooking in the South Pacific and northern Australia. If you are inspired to start cooking with okra greens, then using readily available aibika recipes as inspiration would be a good starting point. That is exactly what I did with this recipe, which turned out to be creamy and delicious. It is great served over rice, and you can substitute any flaky fish or even chicken for the tilapia.

3 bundles okra leaves
2 cans (13.5 fl. oz. / 398 ml each)
    coconut cream
1 tomato, chopped
1 clove garlic, crushed
½ yellow onion, chopped
1 tablespoon mashed ginger
1 teaspoon turmeric powder
½ teaspoon salt
2 tilapia fillets

Remove the okra leaf stems and wash them, tearing the leaves into smaller strips. Heat the coconut cream in a saucepan until it starts to boil. Add the tomato, garlic, onion, ginger, and turmeric. Bring the mixture back to a boil. Add the okra leaves to the mixture along with the salt. Cover with a lid. Leave it to cook for 15 minutes on medium heat. Meanwhile, pan-sear the tilapia in olive oil over medium-high heat for about 4 minutes on each side or until the fish flakes easily with a fork.

Coconut Cream Okra Leaf with Tilapia. *Photograph courtesy of Peter Taylor.*

Old Red Blush. *Photograph courtesy of Peter Taylor.*

CHAPTER 8

Okra Super Seeds

The real substantial food value for this vegetable [okra] is to be found in the ripened seeds, which contain almost as much protein as soybeans, vegetable oil of good quality, an assortment of vitamins and minerals, and some fiber.

—*Unusual Vegetables*, 1978[1]

Eating okra seeds is no special novelty, because everyone who has crunched into an okra pod has consumed them. However, as with so many of the fruits that we eat, the market maturity (the stage at which we like to eat it) of okra pods is quite different from their botanical maturity (when the seeds within are fully formed and capable of germinating). When considering the whole plant, or in this case the whole okra, we must learn not just what parts we can eat, but also when and how those parts are best eaten. Clark Barlowe, an award-winning chef in Charlotte, North Carolina, has been described as the kitchen scrap aficionado. In his own words, "Our farmers are our friends and we take the responsibility of using their products very seriously. To waste any part of it, even something widely recognized as 'trash,' is a disservice to them, and something I cannot bring myself to do."

Chef Barlowe puts this philosophy into practice when he extracts the soft and tender immature seeds from slightly overgrown okra pods for use in a variety of dishes. As is so often the case, though, Barlowe's use of the seeds isn't a new discovery, more of a rediscovery. I came across a 1908 newspaper report about okra seeds that noted, "Sometimes the young seeds are cooked like green peas and sometimes they are boiled and served for a salad with French dressing."[2] As with most things okra, I feel sure there is a deeper link to culinary Africa in the use of the seeds. Barlowe often blanches and freezes the seeds for winter use. He said there is very little difference in character between the fresh and the frozen product, which is a quality he seeks when preserving produce.

When processing overgrown pods to glean the immature seeds, it's hard to resist popping a couple of seeds in your mouth. While I would never steal an experiential lesson from someone unless there was a high chance of death or serious harm, I do offer the warning that in their raw form the seeds can be highly astringent (but not always!). The seeds seem to become more astringent as they age; they are at their tastiest and tenderest when the pods just begin to turn woody. However, even the older, astringent seeds can be dealt with by preparing them in the right way.

According to chef Barlowe the trick is to blanch the seeds in boiling water and then pair them with a fat or an acid. When he makes a cold okra couscous salad, he adds oil, and when he cooks okra seeds with a little stock he adds butter or another fat. If you don't like the astringency of the seeds, try roasting them in a hot oven, or toast them as you would sesame seeds. The crunchy, nutty result works well as a crouton on salads, or is great mixed in with roasted vegetables or crumbled on rice. I brought a bunch of over-grown pods to Sow True Seed and we had a collective pod-shelling break. Workmates took home seeds and extra pods, and the creative minds of my colleagues created okra seed granola (the seeds make an awesome addition to your favorite granola recipe), okra seed hominy (blanched and parched), and okra seed hummus (take care to use the less-astringent seeds!).

Chef Sean Brock has embraced cooking with okra seeds, too, including one creation he described thusly: "Flounder cooked slowly over charcoal, fresh okra seeds (cured in shiro dashi), brown butter sauce thickened with okra slime, tons of lemon." It's awesome to see a southern chef embrace the slime, and curing and marinating the fresh okra seeds opens them up to a whole host of culinary applications. Chef Ian Boden told me that he likes to pickle the seeds and then serve them as an acidic, okra-ey complement with various dishes. Boden uses equal parts white vinegar, apple cider vinegar, and water to make a pickling brine with bay leaves, peppercorns, mustard seeds, salt, and sugar. Based on that idea I've pickled the immature okra seeds in an okra flower vinegar to give a double okra preparation and cele-brate the beautiful pink-red vinegar that okra flowers create. You could also use these seeds to "fill the gaps" when making okra pod pickles.

The fact that these seeds come from pods that are just past their prime is exciting because what to do with woody pods is one of the most common questions/complaints I hear about okra. Now we have a usable and yummy food crop from something previously thought of as compost material. But it gets even better. Once the seeds have been extracted, the remaining pods still

Making the Most of Overgrown Pods

Clark Barlowe shared his process for overgrown okra pods. His first tip was for sourcing the pods if you're not growing your own: "Farmers will have this in abundance in late summer. July and August seem to be our best months for it in North Carolina, but season of availability will vary from region to region. As soon as you see okra at the markets, just put the word out that you are willing to buy any 'overgrown' okra the farmers are willing to sell." If you're growing your own okra then there is a good chance you'll accidentally miss a few pods during harvest and end up with overgrown pods anyway.

STEP 1. If you are processing a large amount of okra, you'll need two large bowls—one to capture seeds and the other to collect de-seeded pods. You'll also want to wear gloves, as the spines can still irritate. Finally, put on a favorite show, or invite some friends to the party; this can take some time.

STEP 2. I like to twist the end of the okra pod so it splits down the seams. Then it's easy to pull the pod apart and run a thumb down the length to scoop out the seeds. Barlowe uses a knife to remove the top and then splits the pod lengthwise. It's a little like shelling beans, but with more seed chambers.

STEP 3. Once you have a pile of seeds, you can preserve them or eat them. Barlowe said, "We typically blanch and freeze all the seeds for fall and winter applications when we would be working more with legumes. For summer applications, you can simply blanch and serve as a couscous substitute hot, or cool the seeds and use them for salads." (See Barlowe's "Okra Seed 'Couscous' Warm Salad" recipe on page 163.)

STEP 4. Dehydrate the remaining pods at 160°F (70°C) for 2–3 days until they're completely dry. Powder the pods in a heavy-duty blender and sift through a fine-mesh strainer. Barlowe said, "We have found this powder offers most of the same thickening properties as cornstarch."

Extracting immature okra seeds from fibrous pods.

have a use in the kitchen. Chef Barlowe dehydrates the de-seeded fibrous pods; when they are fully dry and crunchy, he grinds them into a powder, which he uses as a cornstarch substitute. I really enjoy the flavor of the ground okra pod flour and add it to soups, stews, veggie patties, and anything else that benefits from a little thickening or sticking power. You can even skip the seed-extraction step (which takes a long time) and simply cut the fibrous pods in half lengthwise before dehydrating and powdering them (seeds and all). It makes a delicious, flavorful flour to keep in a jar and use all winter.

As okra pods continue to age, so do the seeds. Seeds gradually lose their tenderness as the exterior hull toughens and thickens. The period from anthesis (when a flower first opens) until full seed maturity is about 40 days. When okra seeds are mature, the pod is completely fibrous and may have turned brown and woody-looking.

University of Texas researcher and chemist Herman J. Kresse became a big proponent of okra seed in the 1970s and patented a machine to mechanically separate the mature seed into its constituent parts: hull, kernel, oil, and germ.[3] "We humans are eating the wrong part of the okra plant to realize the most food potential from it," said Kresse.

Kresse was onto a good thing, but okra seed does not seem to have taken over the culinary world. You can buy bags of hemp seed, chia seed, flaxseed, sunflower seed, and pumpkin seed, but no okra seed. Hemp is perhaps the most similar, with a small kernel inside a tough hull. These seeds are sold as hemp hearts, proclaimed a superfood, and carry a high price tag. Kresse may have been a little early in his okra seed ambitions, but perhaps we'll see okra hearts sprinkled on our morning yogurt in the not-too-distant future? In one newspaper article about Kresse, a photo caption read: "SUPERFOOD? Kresse would like to do for okra seed what George Washington Carver did for the peanut: convert a run-of-the-mill plant into a superfood."[4]

Kresse was not alone in his enthusiasm for the potential of okra seed. According to *Lost Crops of Africa*, volume 2, okra seed is soybean-like with proteins rich in both tryptophan and sulfur-containing amino acids, which is an important combination for combating human malnutrition.[5]

Around the time that Kresse was getting excited about okra in Texas, a Puerto Rican research team was investigating ways that okra seed meal could be used to offset Puerto Rico's reliance on imported wheat grains. Dr. Franklin W. Martin was the lead researcher and served as the director of the Mayaguez Institute of Tropical Agriculture for 20 years. In that time he published many okra-related research papers but was actually considered an expert on rhubarb.

"Rhubarb!" moans Okra.

"Hey, I like rhubarb," I say.

Notice the color and texture differences among the three types of okra flour. *From left to right:* roasted okra seed flour, de-hulled okra seed flour, whole okra pod flour.

"Well why don't you go write a book about it," snaps Okra.

Martin's team was able to grind mature okra seed on a hand-cranked home-style grain mill and sift it to separate the hull from the kernel. This is significant because most of the protein is concentrated in the kernel and not the hull. Their work demonstrated that this is possible on a small scale without requiring patented machinery. The team also baked cookies, cupcakes, and bread containing varying percentages of okra seed meal.

"Best project ever," says Okra.

After reading this report, I ran a bunch of seeds through my Wonder Junior grain mill with the steel burrs set to a fairly loose setting. It was easy to turn the crank, and the seeds cracked through quickly. After the first grind I realized many seeds had partially cracked hulls and still contained the kernels, so I ran everything through a second time on a finer setting. The result was a finer white powder (from the ground kernels) and chunks of cracked hulls, which I separated with a simple metal sifter I found in my kitchen. With very little effort I was left with a bowl of fine white flour that smelled entirely different from the ground roasted seeds, somewhat like freshly ground cornmeal. I think of this product as okra meal. It's definitely a savory flour best used to add a secret okra punch (and some thickening effect) to anything and everything. I've used it to thicken gravies, bind veggie burgers, and bread tofu for baking; a couple of tablespoons have gone into every soup I've made since its discovery.

The Puerto Rican research team conducted lots of different okra seed experiments, including the creation of an okra seed tofu. They followed a fairly simple process used for making traditional tofu from soybeans. Here's how the experimenters described their results: "The okra cheese so produced had a creamy appearance, a smooth texture, a very slight odor, and a pronounced but agreeable flavor similar to tofu from soybean but with a distinctive okra seed flavor."[6]

OKRAVATIONS

What to Do with Woody Pods

As a seed saver and eater, I often leave more pods to go to seed than the average grower. Since it always seems to be November before I get around to splitting open my okra pods to collect the mature seeds, the holiday season is in my thoughts as I create a large stack of beautiful pods. I have experimented with a number of holiday-oriented ideas. *Note*: You can use the pods with the seeds still inside, but if you decide to extract the seeds first then take extra care not to damage the pod.

BASIC ORNAMENTS. Use colored wool or thin twine to wrap the top inch (2.5 cm) or so of the stem end of the pods. Then either tie a loop in the twine or use a paper clip to hang the pods on a tree or mantelpiece. Or they make the craziest earrings. My mum used to own a craft store and she would spray large pinecones with gold and silver paint to use as

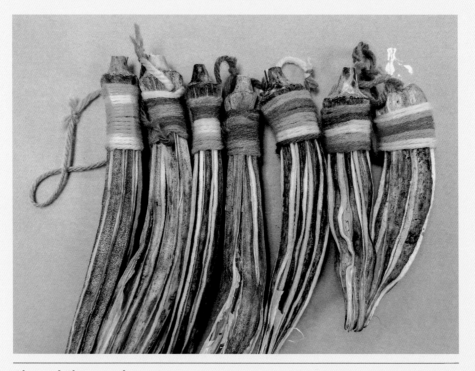

Okra pod Christmas decorations.

hanging ornaments; I think okra pods would lend themselves well to a similar treatment.

LIGHTED PODS. It required some careful cutting, but I was able to remove enough of the dried stem to reveal a hole large enough to insert a small bulb from a string of Christmas lights. The multicolored glows from the already pretty pods was a really cool effect! *Note*: This has not been fire-marshal-approved, and I would only attempt it with LED lights, which don't get very hot.

PAINTED PODS. Emily and I have painted the pods with standard poster paints. It got messy and fun, but the potential for beautiful and artistic was there as well! I've seen pods painted like Father Christmas, with the tip end making a perfect tapered beard.

Outside the holiday season, the pods make great additions to floral decorations.

I have also pasteurized spent pods and inoculated them with oyster mycelium. It took quite some time for the mycelium to colonize the pods, but once it did, I was able to harvest a respectable yield of okra-pod-grown oyster mushrooms. Now, if only I'd thought to cook up those mushrooms with some okra!

Old okra pods inoculated with mycelium.

Okra Seed Tofu and Tempeh

Tofu-making is not in the realm of my experience, so I reached out to Caleb Crowell, who, in his own words, "grew up with hippie parents who owned a tofu business called Bean Mountain in Boone in the late '70s and early '80s." Crowell seemed a natural choice to take on an okra tofu experiment based only on an over-40-year-old reference from a Puerto Rican academic paper. We met in the parking lot of Greenlife and I passed off a jar of mature okra seeds while trying not to look too shady. Two weeks later he emailed with pictures of a block of okra seed tofu!

"Holy moly," I said. "You did it!"

I had a vision of a mad scientist in a lab, lightning flashing, and a plate of okra seed tofu emerging from the swirls of smoke. Crowell's response was much more collected. He wrote, "Made a 200g batch, yielded about 150g of a tofu like substance. The curd was a little bit more delicate than soy bean, but otherwise very similar. Because the curd seemed more delicate I did add lime juice to firm it up, which I have done before with soy. I thought the flavor was better before the lime juice, but it tastes interesting, almost like whole-wheat tofu."

After the successful creation of okra seed tofu, it seemed a natural step to attempt okra seed tempeh. I had read one single-sentence reference to okra seed tempeh in *The Book of Tempeh*,[7] but could find no evidence of it ever being tested. Both tofu and tempeh traditionally use soybeans, although tempeh is already commercially available in many forms. I feel extremely lucky to live in Asheville, where I am surrounded by small artisanal food-centric businesses. I don't know how many American towns have their own tempeh business, but Smiling Hara Tempeh is right down the road and Chad Oliphant, the co-founder, has a history of experimental tempeh (famously, Hempeh). When I reached out, he was happy to talk okra seed tempeh! I visited Smiling Hara's facility in Barnardsville and we chatted about the ins and outs of culturing tempeh. If you've never investigated the creation of tempeh, then it's quite fascinating. Basically tempeh is the intentional molding of a protein source with a specific strain of fungus. This makes the proteins easier to digest as well as creating some delicious flavors. The mycelium (*Rhizopus oryzae*) needs to fully penetrate the seed to tap into the protein and nutrients for growth. This gave rise to the first concern with okra—its thick hull. "Virtually all seed we use for tempeh production is cracked and de-hulled before cooking," Oliphant said.

I left Oliphant with a jar of seeds and a few weeks later received a progress email. Oliphant had boiled the whole okra seeds to soften the hulls and then mashed the seeds with his fingers. He'd set up a few different batches

OKRAVATIONS

Making Okra Seed Tofu

Caleb Crowell explained his process for making okra seed tofu as follows:

STEP 1. Make a seed milk by soaking 200 grams (2½ cups) of okra seeds in 2 liters (8½ cups) of water overnight.

STEP 2. Blend the seeds and the water into a thick milkshake.

STEP 3. Transfer to a pan and heat to 140°F (60°C) (a kitchen thermometer is necessary at this stage).

STEP 4. Strain the slurry through a mesh cloth to make okra seed milk.

STEP 5. This stage uses a coagulant to bind the proteins in the milk, which is when curds are formed. Heat the okra seed milk to 270°F (132°C). Dissolve 2 teaspoons of magnesium chloride (or a coagulant of your choice) in a little warm water and add to the milk. Stir the mixture just a few times and then let it sit.

STEP 6. Curds will form over the next 10 to 20 minutes. Once the curds are formed, strain the liquid and press the curds to form a block. This is traditionally done by scooping the curds into a cheesecloth-lined pressing box. Once all the curds are scooped in, fold the cheesecloth over the top and apply a weight to force the liquid from the curds. The mixture should be weighted until the curds hold together in a block, usually around 20–30 minutes.

Here is the final product: two blocks of okra seed tofu! *Photograph courtesy of Caleb Crowell.*

despite the World Health Organization declaration that the evidence is convincing that consumption of palmitic fatty acids leads to increased risk of cardiovascular disease.[11] The same report noted probable evidence of a decreased risk of cardiovascular disease with consumption of linoleic and oleic acids. However, if you're concerned about heart disease risk, I'd suggest giving up processed foods before worrying about the palmitic acid content of okra seed oil.

Edible homegrown oils had been a side interest of mine well before I read the 1919 report on okra seed oil. Not long afterward I started running okra seeds through my hand-cranked Piteba oil press. I was lucky to have a source of experimental material—old batches of Sow True seed that had failed their germination tests. (Inevitably, the varieties were Clemson Spineless or Red Burgundy because Sow True carries those seeds in larger quantities.) The oil yields were low. It took a lot of effort for a long time to extract an ounce or so of the oil, which was yellowish green, consistent with the description from 100 years ago.

Table 8.1. Fatty acid (% wt.) composition of seven okra varieties

	Myristic	Palmitic	Palmitoleic	Stearic	Oleic	Linoleic	Linolenic
Pusa Sawani	0.5	24.7	2.0	2.2	50.2	20.4	—
Pusa Makhmali	1.0	28.7	0.9	3.7	48.9	16.8	—
Sel-1	0.5	25.3	1.0	3.5	51.0	18.5	0.2
Vaishali Vadhu	trace	25.7	1.6	2.7	47.4	22.8	trace
Clemson Spineless	1.0	22.3	2.0	3.3	50.1	21.3	—
Sel. 6-2	trace	20.3	1.7	5.0	53.3	19.7	trace
Sel. 2-2	0.5	25.8	1.8	2.2	52.2	17.5	trace

Source: B. S. Sohal, "Biochemical Constituents," in Okra Handbook, ed. B. S. Dhankhar and Ram Singh (Palenville, NY: HNB Publishers, 2009).

Table 8.2. Production of seed, oil, and protein by several oilseed crops

Crop	Cultivar	Yield (kg/ha)		
		SEED	PROTEIN	OIL
Sunflower (Helianthus annuus)	Interstate S-7101	224	426	801
Okra (Abelmoschus esculentus)	White Velvet	4677	1169	794
Soybean (Glycine max)	Essex	3360	1008	604
Sesame (Sesamum indicum)	Paloma	1599	671	639
Safflower (Carthamus tinctorius)	S-108	555	222	211

Note: All crops except soybeans were fertilized with nitrogen at the rate of 112 kg/ha annually.

I struggled to figure out how to describe the taste of those early batches, but I couldn't indulge too heavily for lack of quantity. I thought the oil was delicious, but worried the effort of extracting had affected the objectiveness of my palate. I would pass around small samples at my conference presentations on okra, and the feedback from tasters was positive. The oil definitely had a unique and tasty flavor. I would declare that okra seed oil wasn't commercially available, but wouldn't it be wonderful if we did have a regionally grown oil.

"The olive oil of the South?" I would ask rhetorically.

In 2017 Clay Oliver of Oliver Farm in Wilcox County, Georgia, forced me to change my presentation slightly. Clay has been pressing artisanal oils since 2012, offering small-batch, cold-pressed peanut, pecan, sunflower, pumpkin, and benne (sesame) oil. He gained widespread attention for his Green Peanut Oil, winning a Garden and Gun Made in the South food category award in 2015, and a 2016 Good Food Award from the Good Food Foundation, which then got the attention of the *New York Times*. In 2017 he

I use a hand-cranked Piteba oil press to experiment with pressing okra seeds.

Potential Roadblocks for Okra Seeds

It is widely recognized that okra seed, as a flour and oil, has huge potential as a highly nutritious food product. However, that potential has yet to be realized. Available machinery to de-hull the seeds and release the kernel would go a long way toward making okra seed economically viable, and further education to make people aware of the various uses of the seed is critically important. Okra is widely grown across the world. Currently the seed is mainly used for propagation, with a lot of it going to waste each year. I spoke with one seed farmer who said he once had buckets and buckets of okra seed that had been damaged during harvest (by combine) and so failed its germination test. They didn't know what to do with it and eventually composted the entire lot.

Another potential roadblock is the uncertainty over gossypol content and cyclopropene fatty acids (CPE-FAs). Gossypol is most commonly known as a compound found in cottonseed meal and oil. Gossypol has been studied in China and Brazil for its applications as a male contraceptive, but research ceased because of a range of negative side effects. Other medical research has investigated gossypol as an antimalarial and anticancer agent. Its toxicity to humans has led the US Food and Drug Administration to establish a gossypol free tolerance level of 0.045 percent in cottonseed meal.[15] The Food and Agriculture Organization of the United Nations recommends no more than 0.06 percent gossypol for human consumption. Martin authored

another paper specifically focused on gossypol content of vegetable curd made from okra seed (where proteins, oils, and gossypol are concentrated), concluding that their measurements of gossypol were well within the recommended tolerance levels.[16] Further research has clouded the question of gossypol in okra seed, with some suggestion that certain identification methods show a false positive for the presence of gossypol.[17] And more recent analysis suggests okra may not contain gossypol at all.[18] It is clear that gossypol content of okra seed should be considered in future breeding work and varietal trials.

A second concern is the presence of cyclopropene fatty acids, which have been found in plants of the Malvaceae family. CPE-FAs have been tested on animals and reported to cause cancer, atherosclerosis, and death. One study established that the immature seeds of the tested Malvaceae plants had the highest levels of CPE-FAs, which decreased toward maturity.[19] A later study measuring the fatty acids in maturing okra fruits and seeds concluded the opposite, showing no CPE-FAs in the immature fruit or seeds up to 12 days after anthesis, and less than 0.1 percent in the mature dried seeds.[20] A third study then found gossypol and CPE-FAs in common okra but commented that they were lower than in related species within the genus *Abelmoschus*.[21] So, as unsatisfying as it is, we must conclude (and insist) that future breeding work on okra varieties needs to include testing and analysis for gossypol content and CPE-FAs, because the current academic literature is severely lacking.

I did check with Clay Oliver, since he is one of the few people selling an okra seed product. Clay told me he'd spoken with some people from the University of Georgia, who said you'd have to consume gallons of okra seed oil for it to be toxic, at which point gossypol may be the least of your worries. I reached out to the University of Georgia and a researcher cited the articles considered above as suggestive of gossypol and CPE-FAs "not being much of a problem in okra seed consumption." However, most of the university's research focus has been on gossypol in cottonseed meal, not in okra seeds.

Okra Seed Flour

Eating mature okra seeds is far from mainstream, but their potential as a nutritive and medicinal food source is gaining traction in the world of academic research. We could be just one famous person away from the okra seed superfood landslide. A 2011 research paper references the Egyptian use of okra flour to increase the nutritive value of bread, the addition of okra flour to cornmeal in Cameroon, and supplementation of Nigerian ogi with okra flour to increase both micro- and macronutrients. Table 8.1 shows high levels of protein and fat in okra seeds, and in Nigeria okra seed meal is also used to increase the fat and protein contents of weaning food.[22] Another study investigated the fortification of fufu with various proportions of okra seed.[23] Table 8.2 demonstrates an impressive range of amino acids, which supports many of the nutritive and medicinal claims. As a medicine, okra seed has been researched for its adaptogenic anti-stress effects[24] and its high levels of antioxidants.[25] Research into okra seed as treatment for type 2 diabetes[26] supports the traditional Turkish remedy of infusing water with roasted okra seeds.[27]

Table 8.3. Nutritional profile of okra products

Product	Protein (%)	Fat (%)	Fiber (%)
Whole okra grain flour	20.5	14.7	36.9
Dehulled okra grain flour	34.2	25.6	8.7
Roasted okra seed meal	30.3	—	9.5
Whole okra seed	24.2	16.2	23.4
Okra kernels	41.0	30.0	1.5

Source: Victory Preedy, Ronald Watson, and Vinood Patel, *Nuts and Seeds in Health and Disease Prevention* (Cambridge, MA: Academic Press, 2011).

Table 8.4. Amino acid composition of okra products

Amino acid	g/100 g okra seed protein
Aspartic acid	11.57
Threonine	2.86
Serine	5.07
Glutamic acid	15.91
Proline	3.79
Glycine	4.78
Alanine	4.83
Cystine	3.63
Tyrosine	3.46
Arginine	11.17
Histidine	2.34
Isoleucine	2.96
Leucine	6.21
Lysine	6.22
Methionine	1.83
Phenylalanine	4.41
Tryptophan	2.02
Valine	4.24

Source: Victory Preedy, Ronald Watson, and Vinood Patel, *Nuts and Seeds in Health and Disease Prevention* (Cambridge, MA: Academic Press, 2011).

My experiments with okra seed flour began with substituting the rich nutty flour into any recipe I could think of: pancakes, pizza crusts, piecrusts, crackers, waffles, and cookies. I gave some seeds to Sarah Wickers, co-owner of Well Seasoned Table, an herb, spice, and tea company in Candler, North Carolina. Wickers experiments with local and seasonal flavors to create unique blends of salts and spices, so it seemed a natural choice to present her with a big bag of okra seed and a challenge: Make something tasty. She came up with a roasted okra seed sea salt. It is a fairly simple infused salt, but the dark, roasted seeds have a rich, nutty flavor and small amount of crunch. I sprinkle the salt on fried eggs and grilled okra!

As I began to understand its potential as a food source, I recognized the need to connect with somebody who had more expertise with flours and a willingness to experiment. Local baker Maia Surdam met those requirements and more. She is co-owner of OWL Bakery and a fellow board member of Slow Food Asheville. I knew she'd be excited to experiment with okra seed flour. I gave her some okra seeds and a summary of some of the research papers and eagerly awaited her report.

"I wanted to highlight the texture of the okra and also its interesting vegetal flavor, so I decided to go with a savory red pepper and sharp cheddar muffin, which also used a nice gritty cornmeal, an Appalachian variety called Old Yeller," said Maia. "The final result was so good. In fact, I've made them twice!"

I sampled some of these early batches. As instructed by Maia, I cut my sample muffins in half and lightly toasted the halves before devouring both pieces. The muffins had a mild spiciness and so Emily decided she didn't want to try any, which was good because it meant more for me! I was very pleased with myself for getting a professional on board. Still, the process for making the muffins is extremely simple and can be replicated in any home kitchen. Maia also noted that the ground flour seemed to maintain its flavor and smell after being refrigerated for two or three weeks. I think it would be

Maia Surdam shapes the first batch of okra seed sourdough at OWL Bakery.

Okra seed sourdough dipped in okra seed oil. *Photograph courtesy of Peter Taylor.*

possible to grind large batches of flour and freeze them to maintain good flavor. I have a friend who does this with his acorn flour with good results.

"The texture and flavor of the corn and the okra complement each other well," Maia said. "I ended up using the okra flour as about 25 percent of the total flour mixture. I didn't sift the okra flour after grinding it, so there were some larger pieces in there too, which I liked."

Maia applied the same theory with a more ambitious sourdough experiment, using both the coarse and the fine flour in the recipe, "I mixed a bread that was 20 percent okra seed flour with about two-thirds of that finely milled and one-third coarsely milled. As a lover of whole grains, I also included 20 percent whole wheat bread flour and 10 percent cornmeal grits."

I visited the bakery to see the shaping and forming of the dough stage. The dough was pale but speckled with dark okra seed flecks and it had its own special smell, kind of oily and vegetal. Maia was excited about the dough's shape, stretchiness, and smell and commented that it was a good flour to work with. The protein content of okra seed makes the flour good for baking, and it turns out okra also contains sticky gluten, which makes it *great* for bread making.[28]

"I had success on my first round," Maia said. "This bread has a slightly savory flavor, reminiscent of okra, but with more depth. I don't think you'd necessarily guess the secret ingredient without being told beforehand. All the bakers who tried it loved it, and so did our customers who got free samples!"

Okra Seed Coffee

I'm not a prepper (a member of the preparedness movement), but on long drives I often partake in elaborate "what-if" thought experiments of economic, social, and environmental collapse (and the occasional zombie-inspired survivalist fantasy). I'd actually make a terrible prepper. Instead of devising a plan to fulfill fundamental needs, I find myself wondering about simple, daily things like salt, oil, and coffee. Salt is a tough one. I've started buying North Carolinian sea salt and hope trade routes will open in the post-apocalypse. I keep trying to persuade beachgoers to bring me back 5-gallon jugs of saltwater so I can try making my own, so far to no avail. But sourcing coffee will be a real challenge—a challenge that the American South has faced before. On April 19, 1861, President Lincoln ordered a blockade of Confederate seaports, and by 1862 coffee supplies were all but exhausted in the South. Necessity became the mother of invention. Substitutes for coffee were explored before the Civil War, but they became more mainstream during this period.

Charred Okra with Okra Seed Aioli and Crispy Onions

by Chef Ian Boden

SERVES 4

Chef Ian Boden won a StarChefs award for an okra dish that included fried okra leaves and pickled okra seeds. Feel free to apply some Boden flair and garnish this dish in a similar way. This recipe takes some preparation but would be perfect for impressing the crowd at a dinner party—although the mixture of creamy okra seed oil aioli and crunchy okra and onions is so good that you may not want to share. The sliced kumquats are optional, if you happen to be making this dish in kumquat season.

AIOLI

1 egg yolk, room temperature
1 tablespoon white miso
Salt and pepper to taste
1 cup (250 ml) okra seed oil
1 cup (250 ml) neutral oil such as
    grapeseed/canola
¼ cup (60 ml) cider vinegar

CRISPY ONIONS

2 large Spanish onions,
    sliced very thin (preferably
    on a mandoline)
4 cups (960 ml) neutral oil
Salt to taste

CHARRED OKRA

1 pound (453 g) fresh okra
Sea salt
Sliced kumquats (optional)

PREPARING THE AIOLI

Whisk together the yolk, miso, and a pinch of salt and pepper until combined well. Add both oils drop by drop (this takes time; don't rush), whisking constantly until the mixture begins to thicken. If at any time it appears that the oil is not being incorporated, stop adding it and whisk the mixture vigorously until it's smooth, then continue adding oil. Next, whisk in the vinegar until well blended. Whisk in salt to taste. If you prefer, you can prepare the aioli in a food processor by following the same process, but pulsing to combine instead of whisking.

Chill, with the surface covered with plastic wrap, until ready to use.

PREPARING THE ONIONS

Add the sliced onions and all of the oil to a high-sided 2-quart pot and turn the heat to medium-high. Stir the onions and allow them to caramelize; this may take up to 20 minutes. When onions are golden brown, drain the oil through a hand sieve (reserve the oil). Spread the onions on paper towels and season well with salt.

Charred Okra. *Prepared by chef Jamie Swofford, photograph courtesy of Peter Taylor.*

ASSEMBLING THE DISH

Warm a black steel or cast-iron pan on medium-high heat. Put enough of the reserved onion oil in the pan to barely coat the bottom. Add the okra and blister for several minutes on all sides. When the okra is well charred, drain on paper towels and season well with salt. Spread the aioli on the bottom of a serving tray and arrange the okra on top, followed by sliced kumquats (if available), then crispy onions. Serve.

161

Okra Seed "Couscous" Warm Salad. Prepared by chef Clark Barlowe, photograph courtesy of Peter Taylor.

Okra Seed "Couscous" Warm Salad

by Chef Clark Barlowe

SERVES 2

Chef Clark Barlowe is a creative cook, serving meals in his restaurant, Heirloom NC, using produce grown or foraged in North Carolina. As a believer in zero waste, he has gained a reputation as the kitchen-scrap aficionado. This recipe reflects his talent for turning something most farmers would compost (overgrown okra pods) into a gourmet meal (see "Making the Most of Overgrown Pods," page 135). The special touches that Barlowe adds include wild foraged sumac (it grows almost weed-like in North Carolina, but can easily be sourced online), olive oil from Georgia, and lemon balm that grows near the back door of his restaurant.

½ cup (48g) cucumber slices
2 tablespoons fresh lemon balm
½ cup (70 g) feta
2 cups (200 g) immature okra seed
3 tablespoons olive oil
½ teaspoon sumac
½ teaspoon salt
¼ teaspoon finely ground
   black pepper
16–20 small lemon balm leaves,
   for garnish

Slice the cucumber thinly on a mandoline. Chiffonade (finely cut) the fresh lemon balm. Combine the lemon balm chiffonade, feta, and sliced cucumber in medium-sized mixing bowl. Toast the okra "couscous" on medium heat in olive oil for 2–3 minutes or until heated through. Combine the okra with the rest of the ingredients in a mixing bowl and toss to combine. Season with sumac, salt, and black pepper. Garnish with small lemon balm leaves.

Serve warm.

you should not see any unincorporated flour. Cover the dough and allow it to sit for 1 hour.

After the hour has passed, sprinkle the salt over the top of the dough. Sprinkle some water on top of the salt, too—just enough to moisten it and promote absorption. Let it sit for a couple of minutes, then mix, squeezing the dough between your fingers to ensure that the salt is evenly distributed. Cover the dough and let it rest for 30 minutes.

During the next 2 hours, periodically fold the dough gently, allowing 30 minutes' rest between. Wet your hands to prevent the dough from sticking. Using both hands, grab the dough from the top, pulling it up until it does not want to stretch anymore, then fold it down on itself. The fold should cover about two-thirds of the dough mass. Rotate your bowl a quarter turn clockwise and repeat for a total of four folds. When you complete this series of folds, you will notice that the dough will take on more of a ball shape.

After 2 hours and three folding sessions, place the dough in the refrigerator overnight. Keep it in an airtight container so it does not dry out. The dough may rest in the refrigerator between 12 and 18 hours.

The next day, your dough will be ready to bake. Flour a work surface and scrape your dough out onto it. Cut the dough in half (measure by eye or use a scale) and gently shape into two equal rounds. Cover the dough and allow it to rest for 30 minutes.

The final shape of your bread depends on your preference and the materials you have available. If you have access to a Dutch oven or baking stone, you can shape the dough into rounds or batards. (A hearth loaf needs a very hot baking surface combined with steam to bake well.) Let them proof in well-dusted banneton baskets or in linen-lined and flour-dusted bowls. Alternatively, you may do a final pan loaf shape and place the dough in standard bread pans that

have been oiled. For both of these methods, cover the dough loosely with plastic or a towel and let it proof. This may take 1–3 hours.

The bread will rise to fill its container. Gently poke the bread to gauge when it is ready to bake. When the indentation slowly rises back, leaving behind a slight dent, it's ready. If it is underproofed, the bread will bounce right back at you, but if it is overproofed the poke will deflate the gases in the bread. It takes practice and experience to determine exactly when the bread is ready for baking. Remember, even if the bread is over- or underproofed, it will still taste delicious!

For a pan loaf, bake at 450°F (230°C) for about 30 minutes or until the bread reaches an internal temperature of 200°F (93°C). For a hearth loaf, your oven should be preheated to 500°F (260°C), along with the baking stone or Dutch oven. Gently release the bread from its basket onto a piece of parchment paper. The side that had rested in the basket will be the top of the bread. Score the bread using a sharp knife. Slide the parchment and bread onto a hot baking stone, or gently pick it up by the paper and put it into the heated Dutch oven, then place the lid back on top. Creating steam is important. If you use a baking stone, you can put hot water into a shallow pan and place it into the oven along with the bread. If you use the Dutch oven, bake the bread with the lid on for the first 15 minutes to create steam, then remove the lid to finish baking. The bread should bake for about 35 minutes or until it reaches an internal temperature of 200°F (93°C). Alternatively, you may tap on the bottom of the loaf; it should make a hollow thump.

Let the bread cool on a rack before you cut into it. Share and enjoy!

Multigrain Okra Sourdough Bread. *Prepared by baker Maia Surdam, photograph courtesy of Peter Taylor.*

Okra Seed Pancakes. *Photograph courtesy of Peter Taylor.*

Okra Seed Pancakes

by Chris Smith

SERVES 4–6

My family and I have eaten and enjoyed these pancakes for at least three or four years, but in writing this book I realized the need for some external validation that they were actually good. So when Jamie Swofford, chef and farmer, and his food-writer fiancée, Keia Mastrianni, came to stay one evening, I saw my chance. I woke up early the following morning to surprise them with okra seed pancakes. They loved them, or at least they said they did. It occurs to me now that perhaps guests are no more reliable for culinary insight than family . . . Either way, I have since shared these pancakes with enough people that someone would have told me if they were terrible! I often make them dairy-free by substituting almond or oat milk.

1 cup (120 g) okra seed meal

1 cup (100 g) acorn meal or nut flour

1 teaspoon salt

2 teaspoons baking powder

¼ cup (60 ml) vegetable or other neutral-flavored oil

½ cup (170 g) honey

2 eggs

2 cups (500 ml) milk

Preheat a griddle to medium heat. Combine the dry ingredients in a large bowl. (One with a spout is most welcome.) In a second bowl, combine the oil, honey, eggs, and milk and beat well. Add the wet mixture to the dry ingredients in the large bowl. Stir until well mixed. Adjust by adding more milk if the batter appears too thick, more flour if it's too thin. The batter should be thin enough to pour, but not runny.

Drop an experimental dollop of batter onto the griddle. Adjust the heat accordingly. Pour batter using a small ladle onto the griddle, and fry pancakes until the bottoms are browned and the top side bubbles for about 3 minutes. Flip and cook until cakes are barely firm to the touch. Remove the pancakes to a warm plate or hold them in a warm oven, covered with a towel, until you've finished frying all the pancakes. Serve hot.

Lady's Finger—Bhindi. *Photograph courtesy of Peter Taylor.*

CHAPTER 9

Let's Keep Stalking About Okra

The desirability of cultivating multiple-purpose crops cannot be overemphasized, for crops that can produce several kinds of useful products make efficient use of land. The pressure imposed by expanding populations and higher standards of living will force us to produce food, feed, forage, fiber, foliage and fuel on increasingly limited land resources.

—FRANKLIN W. MARTIN, "Okra, Potential Multiple-Purpose Crop for the Temperate Zones and Tropics"

With a stem-to-seed philosophy, instead of recognizing a primary yield and discarding the rest, we rejoice in exploring the widely varied multiple yields that many plants offer us. Okra certainly qualifies, and its uses go beyond the edible.

"I'm more than a mere pod," says Okra.

"That's the spirit," I say. "Look how far you've come from that first family reunion."

"Born again," says Okra.

We can find clues to additional uses of okra by considering some of okra's close relatives: Jute, Kenaf, Roselle, Kapok, and even Cotton. All have been celebrated for their stalks and fibers, and all are members of the Malvaceae (mallow) family. If we dig deeper we begin to see the interconnected web closing in, like the mystical interwoven bast fibers of an okra stalk. *Jute* describes two species of fiber crop, the secondary one being *Corchorus olitorius*, which has an edible green sometimes mistankenly called okra leaf. (*Egyptian spinach*, *molokhia*, and *Jew's mallow* are other common names.)

Joseph Lofthouse Landrace. *Photograph courtesy of Peter Taylor.*

CHAPTER 10

Grow, Okra, Grow

While okra has no great food value, and probably will never become an important commercial crop, a few plants make a desirable addition to the vegetable garden.

—Lee Cleveland Corbett, *Garden Farming*, 1913

Of all the earth's useful plants this is one of the most misunderstood. Taken all round, it likely offers as many production possibilities as ever dreamed in a single plant. However, it also is stuck in a mental warp. Although it holds enough potential to keep a dozen researchers productive for their lifetimes, few are seriously developing it at present.

—Lost Crops of Africa, volume 2, *Vegetables*

Most of this book has explored the exciting life and possibilities of okra, but let's pause here to remember that it all starts and ends with a seed. I think of annual crops as an accelerated version of the cosmic pulsing of our universe, from big bang to big crunch in a single season. The plants explode out of the soil in the spring, miracles happen, and then at the end of the growing season we are left again with a seed. In the case of okra, that seed is the size of a small ball bearing and can feel just as hard. We have high expectations of that seed. First comes the emergence of a hairy root and twin cotyledons; those cotyledons will reach forth as early pioneers, but quickly the first true leaves will follow; at around 3 weeks of age the plant may only be 6 inches (15 cm) tall, but already the taproot can be 18 inches (45 cm) long; by full maturity a 4½-foot (1.4 m) taproot and dense lateral branching that can be 2–3 feet (0.6–0.9 m) in all directions will stabilize and sustain okra; the stem can thicken to the diameter of a soda can and reach heights of 10 feet (3 m) and taller. The lateral branches of some varieties can number in the double digits and also grow beyond reach. At around the 60-day mark, okra starts to flower prolifically, and then the harvest begins—okra will continue to grow, flower and produce pods, filling bushel after bushel, all the way through to a killing frost.

I look at my newborn, Zoe. What did she achieve in her first 60 days?

"I'm a grow-grow-green-growing machine!" says Okra.

Okra is pumped. No matter how many disparaging remarks have been made about eating okra, there is no denying that okra excels in the garden and on the farm. I experienced this firsthand in 2018, when I grew 76 different varieties of okra in order to observe their differences in characteristics and productivity and to provide the fuel for many of the okra experiments I describe in this book. I set up three trial plots in Leicester, North Carolina. The biggest was at Franny's Farm (Franny Tacy is a farmer friend who lives around the corner from me): six plants each of 60 varieties, plus one plant of a 61st variety (don't ask). The second plot was a variety trial of just 10 red varieties at the DiLoreti Family Farms (another set of friends nearby). The third was a small planting of five high-oil-content varieties at my place, Blue and Yellow Makes Farm (but it's really a homestead). When I told people about the trial, the range of responses was quite entertaining. First was shock: "There are *that* many okra varieties?" Yes, it's true. If you haven't worked out the math by now, I can't help you, but there is much more to okra than just Clemson Spineless and Red Burgundy.

Second was disbelief: "But they all look the same, right?" I can empathize with this question because I, too, had wondered if all these varieties were actually subtle iterations of the same basic okra types. But to stroll along the rows of my variety trial plots was to be astounded by diversity.

Third was suspicion: "Why are you doing this?" As if only a madman would contemplate such an undertaking. Fortunately my British accent mitigated this response somewhat, protected by the assumption that I probably didn't know any better.

Maybe I didn't—that was a lot of okra to grow all at once. If you want to know the nitty-gritty details of all the varieties I grew, you can refer to this book's appendix, "Okra Diversity Trial," which lists them all with information about some key traits. I'll also continue to document the varieties I grow and lessons I learn through The Utopian Seed Project, a nonprofit branch of Sow True Seed that explores varietal diversity. In this chapter I'll share all I've learned about okra cultivation, through tending my trial plots and conducting interviews with farmers and experts, to help you grow so much okra that you'll be forced to make okra marshmallows and give them to all your friends.

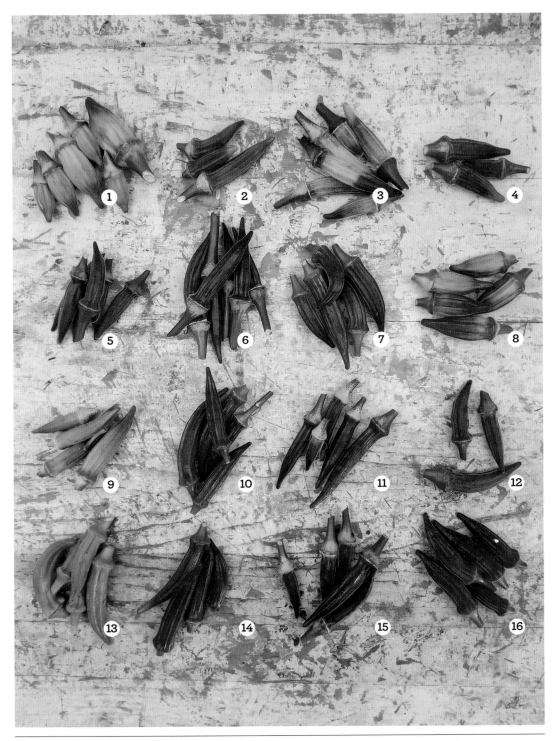

The Reds: **1.** Red Okra 14; **2.** Red Okra 47; **3.** Red Okra 98; **4.** Aunt Hettie's Red; **5.** Bowling Red; **6.** Chatham; **7.** Jing Orange; **8.** Old Red Blush; **9.** Puerto Rico Evergreen; **10.** Purple; **11.** Red Burgundy; **12.** Red Pod; **13.** Red Wonder; **14.** Red Velvet; **15.** Sea Island (Ethiopian Red); **16.** UGA Red.

Germination

Okra seeds have a reputation for being fairly short-lived: 1–3 years viability. A mistake often made is to assume this number is an absolute cutoff. Think of seeds like people. The average life expectancy of an American in 2015 was 78 years old. That doesn't mean that some people won't die much earlier, or that some people won't live much longer; it's just an average of all the lives. In *The Vegetable Garden*, a classic garden reference from 1885, Messieurs Vilmorin and Andrieux list the longevity of seed for various crops and offer two categories of information: "duration of germinating power" and "extreme." For okra the duration of germinating power is 5 years and the extreme is 10 years, which means that some seeds remain viable even after 10 years of storage. Vilmorin-Andrieux's data suggests that the current estimates shared in gardening books and seed catalogs are somewhat conservative.

My approach has always been to store seeds in good conditions (cool, dark, and dry) and to never give up on a seed. If you suspect that you have old seed, you can conduct an informal germination test. This is easily done by soaking 10 seeds in water overnight, then draining the water and placing the seeds on a damp paper towel inside a ziplock bag. Leave the seeds in a warm spot (around 70°F/21°C is fine), and after a few days count how many have sprouted. Two out of 10 seeds equals a 20 percent germination rate; 8 out of 10 equals 80 percent. But even if only 1 out of the 10 germinates, you can still expect 10 seedlings to sprout from a planting of 100 seeds. Those 10 plants will yield a lot of okra and have the potential to produce thousands of seeds. Saving seeds is the best investment you can make—imagine if Wall Street yielded the same returns!

Seed companies are required to conduct germination tests of all varieties they offer for sale, and they can sell only those varieties that meet a minimum germination level. The Code of Federal Regulations, Sec. 201.31 Germination Standards for Vegetable Seeds in Interstate Commerce, lays out the minimum germination standards for a wide range of vegetable crops. The standard for okra is fairly low: Only a 50 percent germination rate is required to pass.

As well as being considered short-lived, okra seed is often described as difficult to germinate. Understanding the nature of the seed and its needs can help address some common germination problems. All seeds require water to germinate, but temperature is also a key factor, and the ideal temperature differs from crop to crop. Sowing seeds in soil of suboptimal temperature can affect both the rate and speed of germination. Table 10.1 shows germination rates and days to emergence at varying temperatures. It is clear that okra likes warm to hot soil.

Table 10.1. Germination rates of okra seed based on time and temperature

Soil temperature	32°F (0°C)	41°F (5°C)	50°F (10°C)	59°F (15°C)	68°F (20°C)	77°F (25°C)	86°F (30°C)	95°F (35°C)	104°F (40°C)
Germination rate	0	0	0	74%	89%	92%	88%	85%	35%
Days to Emerge	—	—	—	27	17	13	7	6	7

Source: Tom Clothier, "Annual/Biennial Seed Germination Database," *Tom Clothier's Garden Walk and Talk,* https://tomclothier.hort.net/page05.html.

When we remember that a seed's main biological imperative is to survive long enough to make more seed, then the soil temperature requirement makes a lot of sense. If okra were to germinate at colder temperatures, then it would run the risk of dying. It's a simple hibernation mechanism. Latency is another component of that hibernation mechanism, which I didn't fully appreciate in okra until I grew Hodnett Special. This is a variety of okra that Sow True Seed had planned to offer for sale, but the crop failed its germination test (46 percent germination). My Sow True Seed colleagues gave me that seed (and some from other low-germinating varieties) for my trials. In the beginning I thought the Hodnett Special seeds were duds. All the other varieties had sprouted and were shooting up, while my row of Hodnett Special remained unbroken black soil. Around that time I stumbled across a letter published in *Mother Earth News* in 1992 and written by Janice Hodnett Faries. It turns out the seed for Hodnett Special had been in the Hodnett family from Rising Star, Texas, since the 1940s and possibly longer. Faries noted, "I do not know much more about this okra other than it takes a long time to germinate (possibly 2–3 weeks . . .)."

Thus, Hodnett Special was no dud. Instead, something within the genetics of that variety slows germination of the seed. That may sound like a useless trait—in our fast-paced, fast-food world we want quick germination, quick growth, quick turnaround. Time is money, people; snap to it!

"Yes *sir*," salutes Okra.

"At ease, soldier," I say. "Remember, I value diversity."

What is valuable about seed that is slow to germinate? Well, in the mountains of western North Carolina, winter can be strangely erratic. Our first frost will generally hit in October, but November can be tropical, and the recent trend of "Februne" (June-like conditions in February) is a real challenge for farmers. Seed that is quick to germinate will break dormancy (hibernation) and sprout during those warm spikes. When winter returns, the tender seedlings will die. Latency is a characteristic of the cunning seed, a seed that is slow to trust. Ideal germination conditions have to be present for a specific period of time before the seed will germinate. While this leads to varieties like Hodnett Special being branded as slow to germinate, it also offers up the exciting potential for self-seeding okra.

Rob Mcelwee, a seed saver from Louisiana, shared with me a story and some pictures of three different patches of naturalized okra growing in the Red River floodplain south of Bossier City and Shreveport (Louisiana). The okra was effectively a weed growing in among corn and cotton fields. Mcelwee thought it was likely the okra had survived on its own since the sharecropper days. He told me, "My grandma remembers the okra at Ninock from as far back as 1943 when my great-grandpa would take her sister-in-law to meet a bus to work at a war plant during WWII." This was the first I had heard of a "wild" okra patch, but Louisiana has mild winters and I wasn't overly surprised. However, shortly after, I met Brian Harris, a farmer in North Carolina, at an event in Durham. Harris told me that okra had naturalized at the edge of one of his fields. He hadn't sown seed for two years and the okra grew to 7½ feet (2.3 m) without assistance, with a 6-foot (1.8 m) spread. Not only was it highly productive, but it was alive and flowering on November 10, which meant it had survived some freezing temperatures. The original okra was a variety called Hill Country Red, but it had surely self-selected for latency and cold tolerance. Imagine if we had wild patches of self-seeding okra scattered throughout our landscapes.

The second challenge to germinating okra seed is the tough exterior seed coat. It's a useful tool for protecting the seed, but it can slow or prevent the germination process. *Scarification* is the term for applying some level of trauma to the exterior of a seed to assist germination, and there is a whole host of gardener's wisdom about scarifying seeds. I love gardener's wisdom because it's rarely consistent from one source to the next and in general it all works. However, the mistake many gardeners make is in assuming that because their way works, then it's the only way, not leaving space for the

Table 10.2. Scarification methods to assess germination time in okra seed

	Hours to first emergence		Hours to 50% emergence	
	CLEMSON SPINELESS	RED BURGUNDY	CLEMSON SPINELESS	RED BURGUNDY
Freeze overnight	24	24	48	48
Bleach 5 minutes	24	12	30	24
Soak 24 hours—cold	24	24	36	30
Soak 8 hours—cold	24	12	24	24
Soak 8 hours—88°F/31°C	12	8	24	24
Germination bag	30	30	48	48

possibility of multiple solutions. I ran side-by-side germination tests to see which of the following common "germination tricks" worked best:

FREEZE. The National Gardening Association advises freezing the seeds overnight for best germination.[1]

BLEACH. Felder Rushing recommends his foolproof method of soaking the seeds in straight bleach for 5 minutes, then rinsing and allowing them to pre-sprout before planting. A common variation of this is to soak in a 10 percent bleach solution overnight.

SOAK. Soaking the seeds prior to planting is a common tip, with many variations on the temperature of the water and the length of the soak. Ira Wallace of Southern Exposure Seed Exchange told me a tepid-water soak definitely helps. Bruce Adams, the farm manager at Furman University in South Carolina, soaks seeds for just a few hours to improve germination.

GERMINATION BAG. Ron Cook, Heavy Hitter okra breeder, places the seeds on a wet paper towel inside a ziplock bag, and then keeps it warm. Cook told me he often puts the ziplock bag in an inside pocket of his jacket. *Note:* All the seeds for my germination trial ended up on a damp paper towel in a germination bag that I left on the kitchen counter. Ron's trick of using body heat would have certainly sped up germination.

PHYSICAL SCARRING. Steffen Mirsky, assistant curator at Seed Savers Exchange (SSE), told me that the SSE staff use nail clippers to nick the seeds and see improvements in germination. I didn't learn this tip until after I conducted my trial, though, so I did not test it.

I tested each method on 40 seeds of two different varieties and noted the time that the first seed germinated and the time that 50 percent of the seeds germinated. Overall, everything germinated rapidly; even the unsoaked seeds showed 50 percent germination within two days. However, seeing the speed of germination of seeds that were soaked for 8 hours, both warm and cold, and the vigor of the seedlings, I would certainly proceed on the recommendation of soaking overnight. The bleach was as effective as eight hours of soaking, but you have to use bleach, so why bother. It would be interesting to replicate this with more varieties, but I'd need a bigger kitchen.

Direct-Seed or Transplant

Direct-seeding is the act of placing a seed directly in the ground. Transplanting is growing the seed in a container (or buying a plant from someone who has) and then transferring the young plant into the ground. Most

Jamie Swofford, the Chef's Farmer, between his rows of roselle and okra, Shelby, North Carolina. *Photograph courtesy of Peter Taylor.*

Wider spacing tends to produce thicker stalks with more lateral branching and more pods per plant than tighter spacing. However, this doesn't necessarily lead to more pods per fixed area. A study on the effect of plant spacing on seed, protein, and oil yield of four okra varieties found that tighter spacing produced more seeds per acre even though seeds per plant was reduced.[6] The study mapped the yield to spacing arc of the four varieties and suggested that six to eight plants per square meter (that's about 3 feet by 3 feet) was the optimal spacing to maximize seed yield for three of the four varieties (Clemson Spineless, Red Okra, and White Velvet). Evergreen Velvet did not fit the pattern and was the only variety whose yields decreased with tighter spacing. The researchers hypothesized that this is due to a basic physiological difference in Evergreen Velvet. Their study serves as an important reminder that there is a huge (and underinvestigated) diversity among okra varieties. A more recent study on plant spacing and its effect on okra growth, pod yield, and yield duration showed that pods per plant and number of leaves decreased as plant density increased, while overall pod yield increased.[7] These studies represent a classic application of the age-old knowledge that I'd rather have a lower percentage of a higher number than a higher percentage of a lower number! Not so important for the home gardener, but critical for the market farmer.

The use of black plastic paired with drip irrigation has become common, especially at larger-scale production where tractor attachments can raise a row, lay drip tape, and cover with plastic in one passing. Ira Wallace of Southern Exposure Seed told me, "Okra definitely likes the soil-warming effect of black plastic." This can be a key strategy for the northern or cooler-weather okra grower, but the plastic also helps with moisture retention and weed control, which is important in okra's early development.[8] Biodegradable plastics are available for sustainable farming systems.[9] Irrigation becomes important with plasticulture because rainfall cannot easily reach the roots and despite okra's ability to survive in drought conditions, its productivity and pod quality are negatively affected without sufficient water.

Harvest

I remember the first time I saw okra in Whole Foods labeled as FANCY OKRA. *Perhaps Jeff Bezos is bringing Whole Foods on board with the okra rebranding effort*, I thought. That's not entirely beyond belief; after all, the *Boston Globe* reported that Bezos ordered crispy duck and stir-fried okra when dining at Sumiao Hunan Kitchen in Boston's Kendall Square.[10] However, it turns out that *fancy okra* is just part of the terminology of a national classification system. The USDA lists general grades and standards for all vegetables, and okra has to pass certain standards before it can be sold.

The USDA established grades for okra back in 1928, with an obvious focus on pod quality. There are separate grades and standards for canned and frozen okra. To meet US No. 1, or Grade A or fancy okra standards, the USDA requires uniform size, good color and freshness, and freedom from disease, damage, and discoloration. In the garden we apply fairly similar standards, albeit less formally. We want to pick tomatoes before they split, corn before it gets chewy, and cucumbers while the seeds are still tender. For okra the main criterion is to pick pods before they turn woody. Most okra varieties are described as "pick when under a certain pod length." And there are a whole host of rules of thumb when it comes to picking okra, including: Pick okra when it's no longer than your thumb!

After picking a lot of okra, you develop a feel for the difference between a tender pod and a fibrous one. There is a subtle softness to the tender pods, which turn rigid with age. This feel does change among varieties, though, so you almost have to learn the crop that you've planted. I've found the shorter, fatter pod shapes much more difficult to tell by feel than the longer pods. Food historian William Woys Weaver has written that visually impaired people are good at picking okra at the right time.[11] I'm not sure if this is based on his personal acquaintances, but the idea that you can tell tender okra by feel certainly holds true. Another okra tip from Weaver comes from his book *Heirloom Vegetable Gardening*: "Take a paring knife into the garden and test a few pods by slicing them in half. If the blade cuts through like soft butter, the pod is ready to cook. If there is resistance, as though cutting through a green apple, the pod is too mature."

A super-useful technique for assessing the woodiness of a pod is the snap trick. Grasp the tip of the pod between your thumb and forefinger and break it off. If the tip snaps off cleanly, then the okra is fresh and tender. If the tip bends or splits, then the pod is already past its prime. This is a good tool to use as you get to know your variety; obviously you don't want to snap the tip off every pod you harvest! Use your ears, too; the slightest sound of splintering wood is cause for concern. John Legare wrote in *The Southern Agriculturist* in 1832: "They are of proper size when two or three inches long; but may be used as long as they remain tender, which is judged of by their brittleness: if good, (that is fit for use) they will snap asunder at the ends, but if they merely bend, they are too old, have become woody, and must be rejected, for a few of such pods will spoil a dish of soup." I'm an optimist at heart and have ruined more than one dish with the flippant thought, *It'll be fine*. It won't be fine; your American family or friends will pull long fibers from their mouths and look at you aghast, while your British family will cough uncontrollably and avoid eye contact for the rest of the meal as okra splinters catch in their throats. However, remember that fibrous pods need not be wasted. You can eat the immature seeds, or dry and grind the whole pods for a winter flour. When harvested young, okra fruits are about 90 percent water. The pods continue their living cycle after

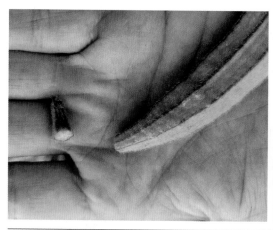

A quick and firm snapping of an okra pod's tip will yield either a clean snap (good to eat) or a splintered snap (too fibrous).

harvest, and as they use up their water reserves, the pods die and decay. Many studies have assessed the best time to pick okra, with 3–9 days after flowering demonstrated as the perfect harvesting interval. I try not to pick okra too young, because I think there is a lot of flavor in the seeds. Really young okra has more of a generic green taste, whereas the nuttier flavors develop later in the pod's development.

Ron Cook, who has grown a lot of okra in his life, said, "Once okra gets going strong, it should be harvested 4 days after bloom set, no matter how long the pod is. The age is what determines toughness. A four-day-old okra pod in rainy weather will grow 6 or 7 inches, but in drought it may only grow 2 inches. After 4 days, it will all be tough, regardless of length."

This is a critical concept to understand. The development of woody fibers is a product of time, not length. It just so happens that increased length is a product of time, too—thus, woodiness and length correlate, but there is no causal relationship. Dry weather and low nighttime temperatures can seriously stunt pod growth, which leads to a 2-inch (5 cm) pod being woody when only the week before the same plant may have been producing 6-inch (15 cm) tender pods. So when a variety description boasts, "Tender at 6"," there should be an asterisk with the caveat, *in ideal conditions*. When looking for varieties that are tender when long, the two traits we want are fast-growing pods and slow-developing fibers. This is the wonderful world of growing your own food, where boilerplate templates can be left in the frozen food aisle. Rather than following standard recommendations, my advice is to get to know the varieties you grow, keep notes, save seeds, and remember that conditions and outcomes will be a little different from year to year.

To maintain maximum freshness, it's important to keep the pods out of direct sunlight right after picking, because the heat hastens the loss of moisture. Keeping pods cool with a high relative humidity is the best way to go, so for the home gardener the refrigerator or a cool basement or root cellar is your best friend. Don't wash pods before storing them; moisture can encourage decay. Be careful not to bruise the pods. Farmers in India use bamboo baskets for bulk packaging of okra because it protects against damaging the pods and helps remove the field heat. Don't underestimate the potency of field heat! I once left a bunch of freshly harvested pods in a cooler for a day, and when I opened the lid I could feel the pods radiating like a stove. In ideal storage conditions good-quality pods will last up to 2 weeks before showing signs of deterioration. Okra does produce small amounts of ethylene during storage.[12] Placing harvested pods in perforated plastic bags to allow airflow helps prevent premature decay. In India zero energy cool chambers (ZECC) constructed out of double walls with a layer

for just a single day, so the whole process from placing the bag to removal takes only about 24 hours. Once the bag is removed, it's important to mark that pod by tying a ribbon or attaching tape or a pipe cleaner to the stem. The marker reminds you that this pod is the seed-saving pod, which contains the pure seed, and all other pods can continue to be harvested and eaten.

I grew only six plants of each variety and I had some concerns about creating a genetic bottleneck (like inbreeding with people), so I saved at least one pod from every single plant. Angie Lavezzo, Sow True Seed's general manager, met me at my okra field at four o'clock one morning and we bagged flowers until sunrise. The eerie predawn quiet woke with the buzzing of insects, the okra flowers opened for a fruitful day of pollination and pod production, but 360 of those flowers were protected from the threat of cross-pollination! If I were growing a larger amount of plants of each variety, I would only save seed from my favorite plants to carry forward the best genetics. What constitutes the best genetics? You can select for whatever is important to you: the most productive plants, or the best branching, best flavor, or most tender, or the plants with the coolest pod color. Edmund Frost, a seed breeder in Virginia, told me that the act of not selecting is still a form of selection, and without human intervention, varieties will drift in their own direction over time (often in a negative direction from a human viewpoint!).

By harvesting pods, you are inducing the plant to produce more pods. Conversely, by leaving pods on the plant, you are in effect causing the plant to send out an internal message to slow down on pod production. Nat Bradford questions this common knowledge, though. "Is that really the case, or is it just something that everyone says?" Bradford asked me. I like being reminded that common knowledge is often untested knowledge, especially in the age of the internet, where repeating "knowledge" to make it common is so easily done. My personal experience offers two conflicting anecdotes. First, when some new seed growers grew okra for Sow True Seed, they experienced terrible yields. We assumed that, in keeping with standard thinking, the plants yielded poorly because the growers let their okra go to seed from the get-go and this caused the plants to stop producing after the first few pods because they'd already achieved their biological imperative. On the other hand, I didn't harvest any pods from my oilseed okra trial because the only product I wanted from those plants was their seeds. I grew about 10 plants of four different varieties and all of them ended up as huge plants laden with pods.

I harvested whole okra stalks to finish drying in my basement. All bundles are labeled for their variety (61 stalks!).

Almost every university extension publication on growing okra notes that failing to continue harvesting pods can cause production to slow down, but I have been unable to find a primary source based on side-by-side trialing. Bradford has piqued my curiosity enough that I plan to run a simple trial to measure overall yield on continually harvested versus non-harvested okra plants. However, I feel confident that allowing a few pods to mature for seed saving is unlikely to have a noticeable effect on production.

I encourage anyone already growing some of their own food to give seed saving a go. It is such a simple, powerful act. My whole okra adventure began with the gifting of a single okra seedpod. Beyond the simple self-sustaining connectivity of seed saving, there are many good reasons to start: It can save money on future seed purchases; it produces a surplus for trade and sharing (and eating); it's an essential component of food security; and it allows for regional adaptation and development of improved cultivars. But seeds represent an even deeper connection. Anyone who loves to read knows that literature has the power to transport us to another time and place. Recipes can do that too. I felt this power with incredible strength and emotion as I prepared okra soup following John Legare's recipe, a recipe written in 1832 that surely encapsulated the knowledge and wisdom of enslaved cooks, who themselves embodied the wisdom of their ancestors and their homeland. In a similar way seeds encapsulate not only a future plant, but also the stories of the places they came from and the people who saved them. Seed saving is the end of a story and the beginning of a story. Seed saving is what makes us cyclical like nature and not linear like the takers in Ishmael's fable. Seeds possess the power to travel through time.

Epilogue

Days are shortening into fall and the harvest has been plentiful—overwhelming at times. How great it is to have a crop that gives so much. On the odd early-morning harvest, when baby Zoe had kept me awake and I felt a little tired, I occasionally allowed myself to think, *Please, Okra, no more.* I didn't really mean it. I dried, I froze, I pickled, I shucked, I ate, I gave, I sold, I donated, I traded a whole lot of okra. I dehydrated enough okra to live off gumbo well into the apocalypse, and there was never a moment when at least three or four household surfaces weren't covered in one okra project or another.

"Try seven or eight," says Belle.

My shelves are filled with jars of dried okra rings, dried okra pods, dried okra flowers, dried okra leaves. My freezer is full of pods cut lengthwise, ready to oil, salt, and oven-roast all winter. Pickles and ferments are lined up in the basement, to offer a taste of summer on cold winter days. Okra stalks are retting in tubs of water for fiber and paper projects later in the winter. Immature seeds extracted from green pods are frozen in jars or preserved in vinegar. The mature wooden pods are beautiful shades of browns and creams; Emily and I will split them open to extract the small seeds inside. They'll be roasted and ground for flour, or pressed for oil, or turned to tempeh and tofu. My seed stock, carefully dried and placed in packets and labeled, is ready for next season. Some of the woody pods have been saved and stored for winter art projects, the greener pods dehydrated and ground into a flour for seasoning and thickening. Flower infusions of vinegar and alcohol sit on my shelves, bright red with memories of summer. Jars and ice cube trays of root mucilage are frozen alongside premade gumbos and soups for quick-fix meals when we're tired and cold.

All this from a single crop in a single year, and already I'm thinking about next season. Why didn't I make an okra flower wine? I wonder if I could perennialize okra in the hoop house? I can't wait to continue my oil-seed okra project. Such is the healthy addiction of growing your own food.

I catch Belle's gaze, and I suspect she is thinking that I should be concentrating on fixing the leaky basement or installing a wood-burning stove, but I know she has come to love okra. So improbable that a British Bloke fell in love with a Southern Belle and inspired her love of okra. At our family table we like to give appreciation. Last night, Emily appreciated dinosaurs and toothbrushes. We hold no judgment. Appreciation should come from the heart and not the head, and okra will always be in our hearts.

"Okra, we appreciate you."

Okra smiles, head held high.

ACKNOWLEDGMENTS

Yon sèl dwèt pa manje kalalou. *A single finger can't eat okra.*

—Haitian proverb

The productivity and potential of okra is matched only by the proliferation of support and help I received along this somewhat crazy book-writing journey. Alex Arnold, who read my entire manuscript and offered excellent editorial advice, wrote, "In case you've lost track of what is normal when it comes to okra, let me remind you that you are deep down the rabbit hole." I'm gratified that I did not go down that rabbit hole alone, or at least I was able to drag a bunch of people with me.

Belle and I met studying creative writing at The University of Manchester, so in addition to the normal familial thanks of patience and support, it was great to have her as a reader. Emmy helped out with okra projects; Zoe is an early riser, but sat quietly most mornings and watched me write, which was a blessing! Carol Koury, the owner of Sow True Seed, has always been a diligent reader of my work. I'm very grateful for all her support. The staff at Sow True Seed were understanding as I took time away to research and write. Special thanks to Sow True Seed's general manager, Angie Lavezzo, who was unerring in her conviction that I *should* spend time writing this book.

In the academic world, Dr. David Shields, Dr. Dave Love, and Dr. Elizabeth Little were extremely supportive with access to research papers.

I am deeply grateful to all the chefs who contributed recipes to this book, but special thanks to chef Clark Barlowe, who let me take over his restaurant, Heirloom NC, for a day to cook all the recipes. Jamie Swofford and chef Steven Goff of Aux Bar both volunteered their time to help me cook. And I am completely amazed at the generosity and support of Peter Taylor, award-winning photographer, who spent the entire day taking many of the incredible photos in this book! That day at Heirloom NC was so much fun and we cooked so much okra, and the photographs are stunning. The other contributing artist I'd like to thank is Amos Kennedy, who creates incredible screen prints and has a range of pro-okra posters (some of which adorn my office!).

I funded my okra variety trial through a successful Kickstarter campaign and am thankful to everyone who was excited about the project and made it happen. Many people helped during the trial, too. Vanessa Chardos and Tiffany Cannoncro (and my parents while visiting from the U.K.!) were regular helpers in the field. I thank Sow True Seed (again), Seed Savers Exchange (SSE), Southern Exposure Seed Exchange (SESE), and Baker Creek Heirloom Seed for sharing their okra collections. This trial was also made possible by the DiLoretis, who let me take over part of their farm and grow a bunch of okra; and Franny Tacy, who allowed me to use part of her growing space at Franny's Farm in Leicester, North Carolina. Financial support from Sow True Seed made this trial a reality as well.

Many thanks to publisher Margo Baldwin for believing in and supporting this project. My editor, Fern Marshall Bradley, has a lot to answer for. She happened to see the first-ever presentation I gave on the topic of okra and suggested to me that it would make a good book, starting the (long) process of achieving my longtime dream of publishing a book. Along the way she and all the Chelsea Green team guided, supported, improved, and generally helped this book become what it is today.

And of course I couldn't have done this without . . . Okra.

APPENDIX

OKRA DIVERSITY TRIAL

In 2018 I grew more okra than I ever had before, by a long shot. In this trial I chose not to include many of the most common okra varieties, not because they were undesirable, but because my aim was to experience, explore, and catalog the wide diversity within the species *Abelmoschus esculentus*. Many people are unaware that such diversity exists, and this trial has only begun to scratch the surface. I have already collected an equal number of completely different varieties for my next trial, and beyond that I know there are many more. As I continue to grow and trial more varieties, I will update and share those experiences via The Utopian Seed Project (www.theutopianseedproject.org), where you can see variety photographs and find additional sourcing and growing information.

In this appendix the "Variety notes" are brief summaries of pertinent information collated from seed companies, seed savers, universities, and researchers. I have included days to harvest where I felt this information was reported consistently and reliably. The "Pod information" and "Trial observations" columns simply record what I observed and learned while growing these varieties in the summer of 2018 in Leicester, North Carolina. My hope is that these notes can offer some insight into okra's vast diversity and encourage you to grow some next season!

Note that I have used abbreviations for the pod information (pod color, pod spininess, and pod shape). Refer to the "Key" to interpret the abbreviations. In some instances I have listed a secondary characteristic in parentheses. For example, Bear Creek Okra is listed as pod color G (Y), meaning it's predominantly green-podded with some pale green or yellow variation. If a variety exhibits distinctly different characteristics among its pods, I've represented that variation with a hyphen. For example, Puerto Rico Evergreen has pod spininess listed as Sm-V-Sp, meaning the variety displayed some smooth pods, some velvety pods, and some spiny pods with no clear dominance.

Variety name	Variety notes
Abigail's Coffee Okra	Tablas, Los Santos, Panama. Joe Simcox discovered this variety being grown by Abigail in Panama, where the locals made a hot beverage from the ground okra seeds.
Alice Elliot	Oklahoma/Missouri heirloom. 80 days. Noted heat and drought tolerance. This variety was brought to Oklahoma from Missouri when the territory was opened for settlement during the Run of 1889.
Aunt Hettie's Red	Tennessee heirloom. 65 days. Grown and saved by Great Aunt Hettie Jane Tidwell (1918–98). Early history unknown. Top 10 in the taste test. Top-tasting red variety.
Bartley Okra	Arkansas heirloom from Hollis, AR. Received from Southern Seed Legacy.
Bear Creek Okra	Missouri. 70 days. A cross of Louisiana Green Velvet, Burgundy, an African variety (name forgotten), and a white okra (name unspecified). Selected for very long, thin fruit with no real ridges over a 15-year period. Top 10 in the taste test.
Beck's Big Buck (aka Snapping Okra)	German heirloom. 57 days. From Malcolm Beck of San Antonio, TX. Noted for vigor. Young pods can be snapped off the plant.
Benoist (Blunt)	Mississippi heirloom. 60 days. Received by SSE from Bill Benoist of Coffeeville, MS. Bill's grandfather W. E. "Buck" Benoist said it was a family okra since the 1880s. A variety threatened by the devastation of Katrina.
Blondy	1986 All-America Selections winner. 50 days. Dwarf, white-podded okra. Early and productive.
Bowling Red	Virginia heirloom. 57 days. Grown by the Bowling family since at least the 1920s. Top variety in the Kerr Center heirloom okra trial in 2008.
Bradford Family	South Carolina heirloom. 60 days. Grown in Sumter, SC, since at least the late 1800s, most likely selected and improved by Nat Bradford's great-grandfather Nathaniel Bradford. Top 10 in the taste test.
Burgundy (aka Red Burgundy)	Bred by Leon Robbins at Clemson University, released 1983. All-America Selections winner, 1988. Noted for its flavor when raw. The most prevalent red variety.
Campbell's Long Green (PI 675126)	Developed in 1940 by Campbell Soup Co. Received seeds from the USDA GRIN. Selection from Perkins Mammoth. Characteristics: slender pod, semi-dwarf, high color.

Appendix

Pod color	Pod spininess	Pod shape	Trial observations
G	Sp	Ri / N	Short plant that struggled at most stages of growth. Low yielding. Insufficient seed produced to experiment with okra seed coffee potential.
G	Sm (Sp)	Ri / N	5–6½' (1.5–2.0 m) green-stemmed plants with red blushing. Pods matured to red.
Rd	Sm	Ri / N	5–8½' (1.5–2.6 m) red-stemmed plants with minor branching. Pods are meatier than most reds. Won the top-tasting red variety.
G	Sm	Ri / N	4–6' (1.2–1.8 m) green-stemmed plants with red blushing. Pods clumped close to main stem for easy and productive harvest.
G (Y)	Sm (Sp)	Ri / N	4–5½' (1.2–1.7 m) green-stemmed plants with red blushing. Minor branching.
G	Sp	Ri / St	7½–8½' (2.3–2.6 m) uniform green-stemmed plants with very minor red blushing. Heavy producer and productive branching.
G (Y)	Sm	Ri / Bi	4½' (1.4 m) green-stemmed plants with minor red tinges. Pods clumped close to main stem for easy and productive harvest. Productive branching.
Y	Sp	Ri / N	4–5' (1.2–1.5 m) green-stemmed plants that reddened with maturity. Heavy lower branch production was a pain to harvest. Some wartiness on pods.
Rd	V	Fl / N	4–5' (1.2–1.5 m) deep-red-stemmed plants. Multiple commenters noted as a low-slime variety.
G (GRb)	Sm	Ri / N	5–6' (1.5–1.8 m) green-stemmed plants with red blushing. Minor branching. Pods clumped close to main stem for easy and productive harvest. Productive. Top 10 finalist in taste test.
R	Sm (Sp)	Ri (Fl) / E	5½' (1.7 m) red-stemmed plants with red petioles and leaves that are red-purple with green blushing.
G (Y)	Sp	Ri / N	5' (1.5 m) green-stemmed plant with red blushing. Moderate branching. Pods were skinny.

Pod color: W = white or very pale green, Y = yellowish or pale green, G = solid green, Gd = dark green, O = orange or light red, R = red, Rd = dark red, GRb = green with red blushing.

Pod spininess: Sm = smooth or spineless, V = velvety or soft hairs, Sp = spiny, VSp = very spiny.

Pod shape: Ro = rounded, Fl = flat sided, Ri = ridged, DRi = deeply ridged, N = normal, St = stubby, Bi = big, E = elongated.

Variety name	Variety notes
Chanchal	India. 50–60 days. High yielding. Highly tolerant to yellow vein mosaic virus (YVMV). Heavy yielder.
Chatham	Seeds received from SSE with limited info.
Cherokee Long Pod	Pods tend to curve and stay tender when long. Noted for its good flavor. This variety could be the same as Grandma Edna's Cherokee Long Pod, which has been in Melba Beasley's family for seven generations and can be traced back to her grandmother Edna, a Cherokee gardener.
Choppee	South Carolina heirloom. 69 days. Maintained by the Jacobs family, Georgetown, SC, since the mid-1800s.
Clemson Spineless	South Carolina heirloom. 56 days. Released by Clemson University and winner of All American Selections award 1939. Top 10 in the taste test.
Dad Speagle's Special Okra	Alabama heirloom. SSE received this variety from Harold Moore, which had been grown by his mother's family since before 1950. Top 10 in the taste test.
Dwarf Green Long Pod	Heirloom. 50 days. The 1920 Landreth Seed Catalog lists: Landreths' Dwarf Stalked Long Green Pod. Most current seed catalogs note its dwarf height (2–3'). Potentially good for northern growers.
Emerald	56 days. Developed by Campbell Soup Co. in 1950. Parentage: Campbell's Long Green, Clemson Spineless, Louisiana Green Velvet, Cow Horn. Thick-walled pods; semi-dwarf, large leaves.
George Sladersky	Arkansas heirloom from Marshall, Searcy County, AR. Received from Southern Seed Legacy.
Gold Coast	50 days. Developed by the Louisiana Agricultural Experimentation Station in 1960. Semi-dwarf (3–4'). SESE notes nematode resistance due to well-developed roots.
Granddaddy's Okra	Texas heirloom. James Gawenis's granddaddy, John H. MacDonald grew the variety in Whitney, TX, after receiving it in 1978. The variety came to John from Rex Eubanks, also of Whitney, whose family had stewarded it for over four generations. Noted for great taste.
Guarijio "Nescafe"	Sonora, Mexico. Native Seed Search notes the plants are very broad and bushy, with large leaves, and are very productive. Seeds can be roasted, ground, and used as a coffee substitute.
Harlow's Homestead	Tennessee heirloom. 75 days. Said to be passed down from the original Tennessee homesteaders and grown for generations. Drought-tolerant.

Appendix

Pod color	Pod spininess	Pod shape	Trial observations
Gd	V	Fl / N	5½–6½' (1.7–2.0 m) skinny green-stemmed plants with red blushing. Minor branching and a tendency to lodge at maturity.
R	V (Sp)	Ri / N	Red-stemmed plant. Purplish pods. Good-looking variety.
G (Y)	Sm	Ri / E	9½' (2.9 m) skinny green-stemmed plants with red blushing. Minor branching. Light green pods blushed red as they aged. Not very productive.
Gd	Sp	Ro / N	3½–5½' (1.1–1.7 m) uniform green-stemmed plant. Moderate but productive branching.
G	V	Ri / N	5–6' (1.5–1.8 m) green-stemmed plants with red blushing. Moderate branching. Pods clumped close to main stem for easy and productive harvest.
Y	Sp	Ri / Bi	3½–4½' (1.1–1.4 m) green-stemmed plants with a pinkish blush at maturity.
G	V (Sp)	Ri / N	5–6' (1.5–1.8 m) green-stemmed plants with red blushing. Distinctly not dwarf-like! Moderate branching.
G	Sp	Ro / E	5–9' (1.5–2.7 m) green-stemmed plants with some red blushing. Minor branching. Pods have a tendency to curl.
Gd	Sp	Ri / N	4½–5' (1.4–1.5 m) green-stemmed plants with red blushing. Moderate branching.
G (GRb)	Sm (Sp)	Ro / Bi	3½–6' (1.1–1.8 m) mix of short and medium green-stemmed plants. Minor branching.
GRb	V	Fl / E	4–5' (1.2–1.5 m) green-stemmed plant with red blushing. Minor branching. Pods have a tendency to curl.
G	Sp	Ri / St	6–7½' (1.8–2.3 m) green-stemmed plants. Small number of tall, productive branches.
G	V	Ri / N	5–6' (1.5–2.0 m) green-stemmed plants with red blushing. Pods clumped close to main stem for easy and productive harvest.

Pod color: W = white or very pale green, Y = yellowish or pale green, G = solid green, Gd = dark green, O = orange or light red, R = red, Rd = dark red, GRb = green with red blushing.

Pod spininess: Sm = smooth or spineless, V = velvety or soft hairs, Sp = spiny, VSp = very spiny.

Pod shape: Ro = rounded, Fl = flat sided, Ri = ridged, DRi = deeply ridged, N = normal, St = stubby, Bi = big, E = elongated.

Variety name	Variety notes
Heavy Hitter	Oklahoma. In the 1990s Ron Cook began saving seeds from Clemson Spineless with a focus on maximum branching and production. Wide spacing needed as plants can reach 8' tall and wide with heavy branching.
Hill Country Red (aka Texas Hill Country)	Texas (mostly limestone Edwards Plateau area of west-central TX) heirloom. 64 days. Brian Harris has a naturalized strain of Hill Country Red that self-seeded in Piedmont, NC.
Hodnett Special	Rising Star, TX, heirloom. Grown by the Hodnett family as early as the 1940s. Noted for its high production and late germination. Top 10 in the taste test.
Hoopers Okra	Graham County, NC, heirloom. Saved by lifetime gardener Clarence Hooper, who received from Claude Hembree, whose family had grown it for over 100 years in Graham and Cherokee Counties.
Jersey Emerald Landrace	Elmer, NJ. Landrace developed by the Experimental Farm Network with the main base genetics coming from Campbell Soup Co.'s Emerald variety. High diversity.
Jing Orange	Asian heirloom. 62 days. Well-known red variety often noted for its ornamental value.
Joseph Lofthouse—Landrace	Paradise, UT. Landrace developed by Joseph Lofthouse from a wide range of varieties to be productive in cooler seasons. Taste test semi-finalist.
Kandahar Pendi	Kandahar, Afghanistan. Originally collected by the little-known but prolific USDA agricultural explorer E. E. Smith in 1954. *Pendi* is simply the name for "okra" in one of the many local languages used in Kandahar. Suited to higher-altitude or cooler-season growing.
Kibbler Family Okra	Prosperity, SC, heirloom. Grown by the Kibbler family for many generations. Experienced grower Jim Kibbler noted that the pods were straight and stayed tender even at 8" or longer. They could be picked with little irritation to the skin. The flavor could not be equaled.
King	Florida. SSE history notes that Cindy Carlson received King okra from her mother in Pensacola, FL. Carlson's mother obtained the variety from a Mr. King.
Lady's Finger—Bhindi	India. Sent to me from a friend in India. Seeds were treated to conform to international shipping standards. Information on packet was generic.
Langston Longhorn	Louisiana heirloom. SSE history notes that Lawrence Langston of Dripping Springs, TX, received the variety from his father-in-law, Albert Clifton of DeQuincy, LA, in about 1975. Clifton got the variety from a friend in DeQuincy in about 1950.

Appendix

Pod color	Pod spininess	Pod shape	Trial observations
GRb	Sm (V)	Ri / N	5½–6½' (1.7–2.0 m) green-stemmed plants with red blushing. Heavily branched. Pods clumped close to main stem for easy and productive harvest.
GRb	Sm (Sp)	Ri / St	Tall plants with high production and beautiful pods.
Y	Sp	Ro / E	8–10' (2.6–3.0 m) green-stemmed plants. Moderate to heavy branching. Very slow to germinate.
G	Sm (V)	Ri / N	6–7' (1.8–2.1 m) green-stemmed plants with red blushing. Moderate to heavy productive branching.
G	V	Fl / N	5½–9' (1.7–2.7 m) varied green-stemmed plants with red blushing. Tall branching. Pods with some warts.
O	V	Ri / N	4–6' (1.2–1.8 m) red-stemmed plants. Moderate and productive branching. Pods are stubbier than many reds with some warts. While not orange, the pods do mature to a lighter/brighter red.
—	—	—	4½–9' (1.4–2.7 m) highly variable plants. "Mixed" is my note in nearly every observational category for this variety.
G (GRb)	Sp (VSp)	Ri / N	3½–9' (1.1–2.7 m) green-stemmed plants with occasional red blushing. Heavily branched. High variance among plants.
G	Sm	Ri / N	5–6' (1.5–1.8 m) green-stemmed plants with red blushing. Moderate branching. Pods clumped close to main stem for easy and productive harvest.
G	Sm (Sp)	Ri / Bi	5–6' (1.5–1.8 m) stout green-stemmed plants with dark red blushing (solid red at maturity). Minor branching. Pods had red blushing at the peduncle.
Gd	Sp	Fl / N	7–9' (2.1–2.7 m) green-stemmed plants with some red blushing. Minor, but productive, branching.
G (Y)	Sp	Ri / Bi	12' (3.7 m) green thick-stemmed plants with red blushing. Large candelabra-like productive branching.

Pod color: W = white or very pale green, Y = yellowish or pale green, G = solid green, Gd = dark green, O = orange or light red, R = red, Rd = dark red, GRb = green with red blushing.

Pod spininess: Sm = smooth or spineless, V = velvety or soft hairs, Sp = spiny, VSp = very spiny.

Pod shape: Ro = rounded, Fl = flat sided, Ri = ridged, DRi = deeply ridged, N = normal, St = stubby, Bi = big, E = elongated.

Variety name	Variety notes
Lee	Arkansas. 54 days. Released by University of Arkansas, 1978. Compact, productive growth.
Little Egypt	Texas. SSE history notes that Ted Gibbs received the variety from Gerald Adaway, TX, in 1983.
Louisiana 16″ Long Pod	Evangeline Parish, LA. Baker Creek reports they received seeds from seed collector Kurt Bridges, who says the plants often get "big like a fir tree" in Louisiana.
Louisiana Green Velvet	Louisiana heirloom. Developed by LSU Agriculture Center. All-American Selections award winner 1941.
Mama Payton's	Georgia/Alabama heirloom. Victory Seeds notes the history of Mama Payton's began when Arthur and Carrie Payton were given seed in 1917 in Cherokee County, AL. They raised this one variety of okra exclusively—a tradition carried on in the Payton family ever since. Taste test semi-finalist.
Mayan	Belize. Baker Creek notes this as a flavorful okra with good-sized pods. This variety was collected by their grower, David Johansen, from an elderly Mayan man in Belize.
Mr. Bill's Big Okra	I collected these seeds at a seed swap in Asheville, NC. They were simply labeled with the variety name.
Old Black Man's Okra (aka Old Red Blush)	I collected these seeds at a seed swap in Chattanooga, TN. They are named because they originally came from an old Black man. I'd like to rename to Old Red Blush, which speaks to the pods' beautiful coloring.
Old German	Heirloom. SSE history notes that Lou Jacobs received the variety circa 1962 from Mr. Lee Jones of Macon, GA. Grown by the Jones family since about 1862.
Perkins Spineless	A Campbell Soup Co. variety released in 1945. Parentage: Campbell's Long Green × Clemson Spineless. Deep-cut leaves, semi-dwarf, early bearing.
Philippine Lady Finger	Philippines. Requires a long growing season.
Puerto Rico Evergreen (PI 209104)	Rio Piedras Experiment Station, Puerto Rico, 1953. Received from USDA GRIN, which notes the collectors as Correll, D. S., Crops Research Division—USDA-ARS; and Miller, J. C., USDA-ARS, Bureau of Plant Industry. 16.4% oil. Early maturity. Top 10 in the taste test.

Appendix

Pod color	Pod spininess	Pod shape	Trial observations
Gd	Sp	Fl / N	5½–7′ (1.7–2.1 m) productive plants with dark green stems and leaves. Minor branching. Pods clumped close to main stem for easy and productive harvest.
Y	VSp	Ri / N	2½′ (0.8 m) green-stemmed plants with pinkish hues. Ground-level branching was highly productive but a pain to harvest (very dense foliage).
Y	VSp	Ri / E	8–10½′ (2.4–3.2 m) green-stemmed plants with dark red blushing. Impressive and productive candelabra branching. Some pods actually matured to 16″. Some red blushing on pods.
G	V (Sp)	Ro / E	8–11′ (2.4–3.4 m) solid green-stemmed plants. Moderate and productive branching.
Y	Sm	Ri / N	10′ (3.0 m) green-stemmed plants with red blushing. Moderate and productive wide candelabra branching.
GRb	V	Ri / N	6′ (1.8 m) stunning red- to green-stemmed plants with beautiful red-green foliage (excellent hedge/ fedge potential). Heavy and productive branching. Unlike any other variety I have seen; I suspect it may not be A. esculentus.
Y	Sp	DRi / St	6½–10′ (2.0–3.0 m) pale-green-stemmed plants. Moderate, wide, candelabra branching that was extremely productive.
GRb	Sp	Ri / St	6–7½′ (1.8–2.3 m) deep-red-stemmed plants. Moderate and highly productive branching. Pods matured to stunning red.
G	Sp	Ri / N	9½′ (2.9 m) green-stemmed plants with red blushing. Productive branching. Pods had a tendency to curl.
Gd	V	Ri / N	4–6′ (1.2–1.8 m) green-stemmed plants with red blushing. Moderate branching.
Gd	Sp	Ro / E	5–6′ (1.5–1.8 m) green-stemmed plants with red blushing. Moderate branching.
G (GRb)	Sm–V–Sp	Ri–Ro / N	9–10′ (2.7–3.0 m) skinny plants with variance in stem color from green- to red-blushed. Minor branching. Variance in pods. Earliest producing and highly productive. Personal favorite.

Pod color: W = white or very pale green, Y = yellowish or pale green, G = solid green, Gd = dark green, O = orange or light red, R = red, Rd = dark red, GRb = green with red blushing.

Pod spininess: Sm = smooth or spineless, V = velvety or soft hairs, Sp = spiny, VSp = very spiny.

Pod shape: Ro = rounded, Fl = flat sided, Ri = ridged, DRi = deeply ridged, N = normal, St = stubby, Bi = big, E = elongated.

Variety name	Variety notes
Purple	Pods have a distinctive, earthy flavor.
Pusa Makhmali (PI 249620)	India. USDA GRIN received seeds from Indian Agricultural Research Institute in 1958. Noted early maturity and 18.3% oilseed content.
Pusa Sawani	New Delhi, India. Very heavy yields and shows good resistance to yellow mosaic.
Rains Okra	Virginia heirloom. SSE history notes that this variety was grown in DeKalb County, AL, by five generations of Dorris Smith's family. Originally grown by Virginia Smith's great-great-grandfather John Rains (1759–1835). Second place in the taste test.
Red Okra 14	Seeds received from SSE with limited info. Likely a Texas heirloom grown at least from the 1950s.
Red Okra 47	Seeds received from SSE with limited info. Potentially originally sourced from Porter & Sons, Seedsmen, in 1979.
Red Okra 98	Cherokee, NC. SSE history notes that Jean Sherwood received seeds from her father-in-law, a retired Baptist minister who is half Cherokee. He was born circa 1915 and indicated that the okra had been in the family a long time, and was grown on the reservation.
Red Pod	Seeds received from SSE with limited info. Possible same variety as Giant Red.
Red Velvet	Origins dating back to the late 19th century, but it's unclear if this Red Velvet (sourced from SSE) shares the phenotype of the historic Red Velvet. It does not display the typical downiness of the velvets.
Red Wonder	Received from SSE with very little info. Research papers note nematode resistance and the use of Red Wonder in a number of breeding lines, including UGA Red.
Rosman Wedding	Received a dried pod of this variety as a gift from a friend who got seeds from a roadside farm stand in Rosman, NC. She had grown those seeds alongside other okra varieties (high chance of cross-pollination) and the dried pod was the progeny of that okra.
Sea Island Variety	Received seeds from Sarah Ross, UGA's Center for Research + Education at Wormsloe, who had received seeds from Sapelo Island seed saving matriarch Cornelia Bailey (now deceased). The seeds were labeled as Ethiopian Red Okra, believed to be a traditional variety of the Gullah Geechee.
Shows Okra	Mississippi heirloom. 58 days. SESE introduced this variety in 2017 and notes that it was named for the Shows family. They received seeds from Texana McFarland, who (in 2017) was 99 and still gardening!

Appendix

Pod color	Pod spininess	Pod shape	Trial observations
R	Sm (Sp)	Ri / N	7–8½′ (2.1–2.6 m) red-stemmed plants. Heavy and productive branching.
Y	Sm	Fl / N	6′ (1.8 m) green-stemmed plants with red blushing. Heavy branching. Highly productive.
G	Sm	Fl / N	7–9′ (2.1–2.7 m) green-stemmed plants with red blushing. Minor branching.
G (GRb)	Sp	Ri / Bi	3–4½′ (0.9–1.4 m) stocky green-stemmed plants with red blushing. Minor branching. Second place in taste test.
GRb	Sm	DRi / St	4–5′ (1.2–1.5 m) red-stemmed plants. Dark green leaves.
R	Sp	Ri / N	5–6′ (1.5–1.8 m) red-stemmed plants. Pods had very shallow ridges.
GRb	Sm	Ri / N	Red-stemmed plant. Standout red variety with gorgeous pods on tall red plants.
R	Sm	Ri / N	3–5′ (0.9–1.5 m) red-stemmed plants.
R	Sp	Ri / N (E)	6–8′ (1.8–2.4 m) red-stemmed plant. Heavy and productive branching with competing leaders.
GRb	V	Ri / N	Green-stemmed plants with red blushing. The truly wondrous thing about this plant is that it wasn't red . . .
G	V	Ri / N	7′ (2.1 m) green-stemmed plants with red blushing. Heavy and productive branching.
R	V	Ri / N	6½–8′ (2.0–2.4 m) dark-red-stemmed plants. Moderate branching.
Y	Sp	Ri / N	4′ (1.2 m) green-stemmed plants. Moderate branching. Some red blushing on pods.

Pod color: W = white or very pale green, Y = yellowish or pale green, G = solid green, Gd = dark green, O = orange or light red, R = red, Rd = dark red, GRb = green with red blushing.

Pod spininess: Sm = smooth or spineless, V = velvety or soft hairs, Sp = spiny, VSp = very spiny.

Pod shape: Ro = rounded, Fl = flat sided, Ri = ridged, DRi = deeply ridged, N = normal, St = stubby, Bi = big, E = elongated.

Variety name	Variety notes
Silver Queen	Heirloom. 57 days. Highly productive and renowned for its flavor. A true white okra.
Stelley Okra	St. Landry Parish, LA, heirloom. Baker Creek received seeds from Kurt Bridges who found the seed growing near an old homestead abandoned 50 years ago!
Stewart's Zeebest	Houston, TX, 1980s. 57 days. Developed by George and Mary Stewart for branching and a tender smooth-podded okra (original parent: LA Green Velvet). Mary Stewart noted they achieved a plant with 28 branches and 243 pods on it at one time as a result of nine years of selection.
Stubby	Texas/Louisiana heirloom. SSE history notes that they received it from William Woys Weaver (PA), who acquired this variety in 1995 from Laurent Hodges (IA). Hodges stated that it is a family heirloom.
UGA Red	Georgia. This variety was originally developed and released by the University of Georgia in 1985. Will Corley states that he developed UGA Red from a cross between Red Wonder and Dwarf Green Long Pod with the intention of creating an edible ornamental.
Whidley White	Heirloom. Limited varietal information. SSE history notes that Mrs. H. L. Jarrard of Georgia was the original donor. Reportedly grown since the mid-1800s by a single family.
White Satin	Montgomery County, NC. David Goforth passed seeds to me as White Satin, which he received from his mom, Alvis Poole Goforth, and she received from her mom, Stella Kelly Poole.
White Velvet	Heirloom. 65 days. Included on the Slow Food USA Ark of Taste. White okra was historically enjoyed and preferred across the South and especially in Alabama. Registered and commercially introduced to the public in 1890 by Peter Henderson & Company of New York.
Yalova Akköy (aka Sultani)	Turkey. Two Seeds In A Pod Heirloom Seed Co. introduced this variety from Turkey, noting that it is one of the most popular Turkish varieties.

Pod color	Pod spininess	Pod shape	Trial observations
W	Sp	Ro / Bi	6–7′ (1.8–2.1 m) green-stemmed plants. Moderate but thick and productive branching. Pods displayed some extremely shallow ridges.
G	Sm (Sp)	Ri / N	9–11′ (2.7–3.4 m) green-stemmed plants with red branching. Stout candelabra branching. High longevity.
Gd	Sp	Ro / E	6–7′ (1.8–2.1 m) dark-green-stemmed plants with some minor red blushing. Moderate branching.
G	V (Sp)	Ri / St	7–8′ (2.1–2.4 m) green-stemmed plants with minor red blush. Productive candelabra branching. Pods were short with very chunky peduncle.
R	Sm (Sp)	DRi / N	5–6′ (1.5–1.8 m) red-stemmed plants. Heavy and productive branching. Some warty pods and some with green blushing.
W-Y-G	Sp	Fl-Ri / Bi	Short plants. High variance in pod type and color. Selected for white pods with no warts with plans for further selections to bring this variety back on track.
Y (W)	Sm (Sp)	Ri / N	5½′ (1.7 m) pale-green-stemmed plants with red blushing. Moderate branching.
Y	V	Ro / N	6–7′ (1.8–2.1 m) green-stemmed plants with red blushing. Minor branching. Pods were greener than expected and displayed some red blushing (varietal drift?).
Y	V-Sp	Fl-Ri / N	4–10′ (1.2–3.0 m) green-stemmed plants some with red blushing. Minor to moderate branching. Wide variance in plants and pods. Turkish landrace? Low production. Winner of the taste test.

Pod color: W = white or very pale green, Y = yellowish or pale green, G = solid green, Gd = dark green, O = orange or light red, R = red, Rd = dark red, GRb = green with red blushing.

Pod spininess: Sm = smooth or spineless, V = velvety or soft hairs, Sp = spiny, VSp = very spiny.

Pod shape: Ro = rounded, Fl = flat sided, Ri = ridged, DRi = deeply ridged, N = normal, St = stubby, Bi = big, E = elongated.

NOTES

Introduction. In Defense of Okra

1. Dick West, "In Defense of Okra," UPI, October 14, 1964.
2. Molefi Kete Asante and Ama Mazama, eds., *Encyclopedia of African Religion* (Thousand Oaks, CA: Sage Publications, 2008).
3. Roy Blount Jr., "Mad About Okra," *Garden & Gun*, October–November 2012.

Chapter 1. Getting to Know Okra

1. Kim Severson, "Okra's Triumph of Taste Over Texture," *New York Times*, August 25, 2014, https://www.nytimes.com/2014/08/27/dining/okras-triumph-of -taste-over-texture.html.
2. Edward Lewine, "At Home with Tom Colicchio," *New York Times Magazine*, April 29, 2009, https://www.nytimes.com/2009/05/03/magazine/03wwln -domains-t.html.
3. Barbara Wilde, "Okra, North and South," *Organic Gardening*, June 2006.
4. Julia Reed, "Food; Turning Green," *New York Times Magazine*, October 13, 2002.
5. National Research Council, *Lost Crops of Africa*, vol. 2, *Vegetables* (Washington, DC: National Academies Press, 2006).
6. K. K. Tripathi et al., *Biology of Abelmoschus esculentus (Okra)* (New Delhi: Department of Biotechnology, Ministry of Science and Technology, and Ministry of Environment and Forests, Government of India, 2011).
7. "Okra," in *Encyclopædia Britannica: A Dictionary of Arts, Sciences, Literature and General Information*, vol. 12 (Cambridge, U.K.: Cambridge University Press, 1911).
8. Friedrich Fluckiger and Daniel Hanbury, *Pharmacographia: A History of the Principal Drugs of Vegetable Origin Met with in Great Britain and British India* (London: Macmillan, 1879).
9. N. I. Vavilov, "The Origin, Variation, Immunity and Breeding of Cultivated Plants (Eng. trans. by K. S. Chester, 1951)," *Chronica Botanica* 13 (1950).
10. P. Aschersonand and G. Schweinfurth, *Illustration de la Flore D'Egypte* (Cairo: D. D. Fouquet, 1889).
11. B. S. Dhankhar and J. P. Mishra, "Origin, History, and Distribution," in *Okra Handbook*, ed. B. S. Dhankhar and Ram Singh (Palenville, NY: HNB Publishing, 2009).
12. Nerkar, Y. S., and Jambhale, N. D. "Taxonomy, Cytology and Evolution" in *Okra Handbook*, ed. Dhankhar and Singh.
13. J. S. Siemonsma, "West African Okra—Morphological and Cytogenetical Indications for the Existence of a Natural Amphiploid of *Abelmoschus esculentus* (L.) Moench and *A. manihot* (L). Medikus," *Euphytica* 31, no. 1 (1982): 241–52.

14. S. Kahlheberand and K. Neumann, "The Development of Plant Cultivation in Semi-Arid West Africa," in *Rethinking Agriculture: Archaeological and Ethnoarchaeological Perspectives*, ed. T. P. Denham, J. Iriarte, and L. L. Vrydaghs (Walnut Creek, CA: Left Coast Press, 2007).

15. M. E. Osawaruand and F. M. Dania-Ogbe, "Ethnobotanical Studies of West African Okra [*Abelmoschus caillei* (A. Chev) Stevels] from Some Tribes of South Western Nigeria," *Science World Journal* 5, no. 1 (2010): 36–41.

16. Jessica Carney and R. N. Rosomoff, *In the Shadow of Slavery: Africa's Botanical Legacy in the Atlantic World* (Berkeley: University of California Press, 2010).

17. Peter Kalm, *Peter Kalm's Travels in North America: The English Version of 1770* (Mineola, NY: Dover, 1987).

18. Luigi Catiglioni, *Luigi Castiglioni's Viaggio: Travels in the United States of North America, 1785–1787* (Sycracuse, NY: Sycracuse University Press, 1983).

19. Hugh Crow, *Memoirs of the Late Captain Hugh Crow of Liverpool, Comprising a Narrative of His Life, Together with Descriptive Sketches of Africa, Particularly of Bonny, the Manners and Customs of the Inhabitants, the Production of the Soil, and the Trade of the Country, to Which Are Added Anecdotes and Observations of the Negro Character* (London: F. Cass, 1970).

20. Jessica Harris, "In Praise of Okra," *Zester Daily*, July 7, 2010.

21. Leah Penniman, *Farming While Black: Soul Fire Farm's Practical Guide to Liberation of the Land* (White River Junction, VT: Chelsea Green Publishing, 2018).

22. Michael W. Twitty, "The Secret History of Okra—Okra Soup," *Tori Avey* (blog), August 13, 2018, https://toriavey.com/history-kitchen/history-okra-soup-recipe.

23. Twitty, "The Secret History of Okra—Okra Soup."

24. Koen Bostoen and Joseph Koni Muluwa, "Were the First Bantu Speakers South of the Rainforest Farmers? A First Assessment of the Linguistic Evidence," in *Language Dispersal Beyond Farming*, ed. Martine Robbeets and Alexander Savelyev (Amsterdam: John Benjamins, 2017), 235–58.

Chapter 2. Okra, The People's Vegetable

1. Dick West, "Okra Plant Handed Role of Underdog," UPI, October 13, 1964.

2. R. S. Rana, *Report of an International Workshop on Okra Genetic Resources* (Rome: International Board for Plant Genetic Resources, 1991).

3. Habtamu Fekadu Gemede et al., "Nutritional Quality and Health Benefits of Okra (*Abelmoschus esculentus*): A Review," *Food Science and Quality Management* 33 (2014): 87.

4. ErikaYigzaw, "10 Green Superfoods Your Holistic Nutritionist Eats," *ACHS Holistic Health and Wellness Blog*, March 16, 2018, http://info.achs.edu/blog/bid/339438/10-green-superfoods-your-holistic-nutritionist-eats.

5. L. Panneerselvam et al., "Antidiabetic and Antihyperlipidemic Potential of *Abelmoschus esculentus* (L.) Moench in Streptozotocin-Induced Diabetic Rats," *Journal of Pharmacy and Bioallied Sciences* 3, no. 3 (2011): 397–402.

6. Habtamu Fekadu Gemede et al., "Nutritional Quality and Health Benefits of Okra (*Abelmoschus esculentus*): A Review," *Journal of Food Processing and Technology*, December 27, 2016.

7. Leonardo G. Monte et al., "Lectin of *Abelmoschus esculentus* (Okra) Promotes Selective Antitumor Effects in Human Breast Cancer Cells," *Biotechnology Letters* 36, no. 3 (2013): 461–69.

8. David J. Jenkins et al., "Direct Comparison of a Dietary Portfolio of Cholesterol-Lowering Foods with a Statin in Hypercholesterolemic Participants," *American Journal of Clinical Nutrition* 81, no. 2 (2005): 380–87.

9. Alexandra Sifferlin, "Eat This Now: Okra," *Time*, July 22, 2013, http://healthland.time.com/2013/07/22/eat-this-now-okra.

10. Constantine Samuel Rafinesque, *Medical Flora; Or, Manual of the Medical Botany of the United States of North America: Containing a Selection of Above 100 Figures and Descriptions of Medical Plants, with Their Names, Qualities, Properties, History, &c.: and Notes or Remarks on Nearly 500 Equivalent Substitutes* (Philadelphia: Atkinson & Alexander, 1830).

11. H. A. Woodle, "Aiken County Farm Flashes," *Aiken (SC) Standard*, March 3, 1939.

12. "'Clemson Spineless' New Okra Developed," *Gaffney (SC) Ledger*, March 11, 1937, 6.

13. "Okra," *Genesee Farmer and Gardener's Journal*, March 17, 1832.

14. Carol Deppee, *Breed Your Own Vegetable Varieties: The Gardener's and Farmer's Guide to Plant Breeding and Seed Breeding* (White River Junction, VT: Chelsea Green Publishing, 2000).

15. "What's on the Menu?," Waldorf-Astoria, October 4, 1912, http://menus.nypl.org/menus/34896.

16. W. R. Beattie, *Okra: Its Culture and Uses* (Washington, DC: US Department of Agriculture, 1905).

17. "The Country Women's Corner," *Troy (AL) Messenger*, August 30, 1916.

Chapter 3. Embracing the S-Word

1. Jessica Harris, "Okra," *Africooks: Literary Works and Beyond* (blog), March 1, 2017, http://www.africooks.com/wordpress/?p=81.

2. "FAOSTAT," Food and Agriculture Organization of the United Nations, http://www.fao.org/faostat.

3. "Slimy," in *The Oxford Pocket Dictionary of Current English* (Oxford, U.K.: Oxford University Press, 2009).

4. W. R. Beattie, *Okra: Its Culture and Uses*.

5. Victor R. Boswell, "Our Vegetable Travelers," *National Geographic Magazine*, August 1949.

6. W. R. Beattie, *Okra: Its Culture and Uses*.

7. Jon P. Weimer and Patricia Stevens, *Consumers' Preferences, Uses, and Buying Practices for Selected Vegetables: A Nationwide Survey* (Washington, DC: USDA Economic Research Service, 1974).

8. "America's Most Hated Food," *AOL Food*, June 30, 2008, http://food.aol.com/dinner-tonight/most-hated-foods.

9. Vertamae Grosvenor, "Memories of Southern Chef Edna Lewis," NPR, February 17, 2006.

10. Michael W. Twitty, *The Cooking Gene: A Journey Through African American Culinary History in the Old South* (New York: HarperCollins Publishers, 2017).

11. Vadhera Shalini, *Passport to Beauty: Secrets and Tips from Around the World for Becoming a Global Goddess* (New York: St. Martin's Press, 2006).

12. Anupam Roy, Shanker Lal Shrivastava, and Santi M. Manda, "Functional Properties of Okra *Abelmoschus esculentus* L. (Moench): Traditional Claims and Scientific Evidences," *Plant Science Today* 1, no. 3 (2014): 121–30.

13. Nitin Sharma et al., "Development of *Abelmoschus esculentus* (Okra)–Based Mucoadhesive Gel for Nasal Delivery of Rizatriptan Benzoate," *Tropical Journal of Pharmaceutical Research* 12, no. 2 (2013): 149–53.

14. Carla de Carvalho et al., "Antibacterial Properties of the Extract of *Abelmoschus esculentus*," *Biotechnology and Bioprocess Engineering* 16, no. 5 (2011): 971–77.

15. H. B. Benjamin, H. K. Ihrig, and D. A. Roth, "The Use of Okra as a Plasma Replacement," *Revue Canadienne de Biologie* 10, no. 3 (1951): 215–21.

16. W. E. Castro et al., "Reducing Fluid Friction with Okra," *Chemical Technology* 1 (1971): 697–701.

17. Ikoni Ogaji and Obiageli Nnoli, "Film Coating Potential of Okra Gum Using Paracetamol Tablets as a Model Drug," *Asian Journal of Pharmaceutics* 4, no. 2 (2010).

18. William Saenz, "Some Applications of Okra in the Food Industries," *Florida State Horticultural Society* 73 (1960): 297–301.

19. M. de Alvarenga Pinto Cotrim, A. C. Mottin, and E. Ayres, "Preparation and Characterization of Okra Mucilage (*Abelmoschus esculentus*) Edible Films," *Macromolecular Symposia* 367 (2016): 90–100.

20. Mark L. Woolfe, Martin F. Chaplid, and Gifty Otchere, "Studies on the Mucilages Extracted from Okra Fruits (*Hibiscus esculentus* L.) and Baobab Leaves (*Adansonia digitata* L.)," *Journal of the Science of Food and Agriculture* 28, no. 6 (1977): 519–29.

21. Ema Sagner, "The Rise of the Slime Economy," NPR, October 1, 2017.

22. Woolfe, Chaplid, and Otchere, "Studies on the Mucilages Extracted from Okra Fruits."

Chapter 4. Pods of the Gods

1. "Brunswick Stew," *Table Talk* 21 (1906): 267.

2. Emily Horton, "Think You Hate Okra? These Slime-Cutting Techniques Will Change Your Mind," *Washington Post*, September 5, 2018.

3. Cynthia LeJeune Nobles, "Gumbo," in *New Orleans Cuisine: Fourteen Signature Dishes and Their Histories* (Jackson: University Press of Mississippi, 2009).

4. From *Observations sur la physique, sur l'histoire naturelle et sur les arts*, published in 1788. This book quotes a certain Monsieur P. de la Coudrenière, author of a short tract titled (in translation) "Observations on the Sassafras, Tree of America."

5. Albert Valdman, *Dictionary of Louisiana Creole* (Bloomington: Indiana University Press, 1998).

6. Bostoen and Muluwa, "Were the First Bantu Speakers South of the Rainforest Farmers?"

7. Karen Pinchin, "How Slaves Shaped American Cooking," *National Geographic*, March 1, 2014, https://news.nationalgeographic.com/news/2014/03/140301 -african-american-food-history-slavery-south-cuisine-chefs.

8. Catherine Zuckerman, "5 African Foods You Thought Were American," *National Geographic*, September 21, 2016, https://www.nationalgeographic.com/people -and-culture/food/the-plate/2016/09/5-foods-from-africa.

9. Twitty, "The Secret History of Okra—Okra Soup."

10. John Legare, "Part III, Miscellaneous Intelligence," *The Southern Agriculturist*, August 1831.

11. Pinchin, "How Slaves Shaped American Cooking."

12. Lolis Eric Elie, "The Origin Myth of New Orleans Cuisine," *Oxford American*, April 3, 2010, https://www.oxfordamerican.org/magazine/item/206-lolis-eric -elie-explores-the-origin-myth-of-new-orleans-cuisine.

13. "Interrogation of Julia (Comba)," Records of the French Superior Council, Louisiana Historical Center, New Orleans, September 4, 1764.

14. Katherine Preston, "Okra—What's Not to Like?," *The Botanist in the Kitchen*, June 17, 2014, https://botanistinthekitchen.blog/2013/09/21/okra-whats -not-to-like.

15. Noorlaila Ahmad et al., "Emulsifying Properties of Extracted Okra (*Abelmoschus esculentus* L.) Mucilage of Different Maturity Index and Its Application in Coconut Milk Emulsion," *International Food Research Journal* 22, no. 2 (2015): 782–87.

16. "Okra," *The Southern Planter* 17, no. 8 (1857): 462.

17. *Timely Suggestions for Homekeepers, Menu, and Tested Recipes* (Washington, DC: US Department of Agriculture, 1928).

Chapter 5. How to Eat Okra All Winter

1. Erin Huffstetler, "Homemade Fruit and Vegetable Wash," *The Spruce Eats* (blog), November 24, 2018, https://www.thespruceeats.com/homemade-fruit-and -vegetable-wash-1387935.

2. "An Okra Evaporator," *Weekly Advertizer*, August 3, 1900.

3. W. R. Beattie, *Okra: Its Culture and Uses*.

4. A. J. Farinde, O. K. Owolarafe, and O. I. Ogungbemi, "An Overview of Production, Processing, Marketing and Utilisation of Okra in Egbedore Local Government Area of Osun State, Nigeria," *Journal of Agronomy* 4, no. 2 (2006): 342–49.

5. Gullah Geechee Cultural Heritage Corridor Commission, *2012 Gullah Geechee Cultural Heritage Corridor Management Plan* (Denver, CO: National Park Service, Denver Service Center, 2012).

6. National Research Council, *Lost Crops of Africa*, vol. 2, *Vegetables*.

7. US Bureau of Plant Industry, *Inventory, Plant Material Introduced* (Washington, DC: US Government Printing Office, 1912).

Chapter 6. Take the Okra Flower Pledge

1. Hans R. Dhingra, "Morphological Features and Reproductive Biology," in *Okra Handbook*, ed. Dhankhar and Singh.

2. S. S. Purewal and G. S. Randhawa, "Studies in *Hibiscus esculentus* (Lady's Finger): Chromosome and Pollination Studies," *Indian Journal of Agricultural Science* 17 (1947): 129–36.

3. M. T. Njoya, D. Wittmann, and M. Schindler, "Effect of Bee Pollination on Seed Set and Nutrition on Okra (*Abelmoschus esculentus*) in Cameroon" (presentation, The Global Food and Product Chain: Dynamics, Innovations, Conflicts, Strategies, Hohenheim, Germany, October 11–13, 2005).

4. A. A. Al-Ghzawi, "The Impact of Wild Bees on the Pollination of Eight Okra Genotypes Under Semi-Arid Mediterranean Conditions," *International Journal of Agriculture and Biology* 5 (2003): 408–10.

5. Charles D. Michener, *Bees of the World* (Baltimore: John Hopkins University Press, 2007).

6. Hans R. Dhingra, "Morphological Features and Reproductive Biology."

7. Otakar Rop et al., "Edible Flowers: A New Promising Source of Mineral Elements in Human Nutrition," *Molecules* 17, no. 6 (2012): 6672–83.

8. H. Z. Gu and J. B. Song, "Progress of Studies on *Abelmoschus manihot* (L.)," *Medical Journal of Chinese Medicine Materials* 21 (1998): 158–60.

9. M. M. Onakpa, "Ethnomedicinal, Phytochemical and Pharmacological Profile of Genus *Abelmoschus*," *Phytopharmacology* 4, no. 3 (2013): 648–63.

10. B. S. Dhillon, ed., *Plant Genetic Resources: Horticulural Crops* (Oxford, U.K.: Alpha Science International, 2005).

Chapter 7. Eat Your Greens

1. "Rival for Cotton Has Been Found," *Vicksburg (MS) Evening Post*, October 15, 1907.

2. P. R. Mayagüez, *Vegetables for the Hot, Humid Tropics* (New Orleans: US Agricultural Research Service, 1977).

3. Anand P. Tyagi, "Aibika (*Abelmoschus manihot*): A Leafy Vegetable in Asia-Pacific," in *Okra Handbook*, ed. Dhankhar and Singh.

4. Graham Lyons and Mary Taylor, *Feasibility Study on Increasing the Consumption of Nutritionally-Rich Leafy Vegetables by Indigenous Communities in Samoa, Solomon Islands and Northern Australia* (Bruce, Australia: Australian Centre for International Agricultural Research, 2015).

5. Lyons and Taylor, *Feasibility Study*.

6. "PNG Traditional Vegetables Project," http://traditionalvegetables.cdu.edu.au.

Chapter 8. Okra Super Seeds

1. Anne Moyer Halpin, ed., *Unusual Vegetables: Something New for This Year's Garden* (Emmaus, PA: Rodale Press, 1978).

2. Emma Paddock Telford, "The Valueable and Nutritious Okra," *Burlington (VT) Free Press*, September 8, 1908.

3. Herman J. Kresse, "Separation of Mature Okra Seed into Component Fractions," US Patent 4059604, issued November 22, 1977.

4. "Okra Seed Is Studied for a Variety of Uses," *Desert Sun* (CA), November 20, 1976.

5. National Research Council, *Lost Crops of Africa*, vol. 2, *Vegetables*.

6. Franklin Martin and Ruth Ruberté, "Milling and Use of Okra Seed Meal at the Household Level," *Journal of Agriculture of the University of Puerto Rico* (1979): 1–7.

7. William Shurtleff and Akiko Aoyagi, *The Book of Tempeh*, vol. 1 (Lafayette, CA: Soyinfo Center, 1979).

8. "Items," *Cincinnati Daily Gazette*, October 6, 1874.

9. George S. Jamieson and Walter E. Baughman, "Okra Seed Oil," *Journal of the American Chemical Society* 42, no. 1 (1920): 166–70.

10. B. S. Sohal, "Biochemical Constituents," in *Okra Handbook*, ed. Dhankhar and Singh.

11. *Diet, Nutrition and the Prevention of Chronic Diseases*, WHO Technical Report Series 916 (Geneva: World Health Organization, 2003).

12. Robert L. Jarret, "Seed Oil and Fatty Acid Content in Okra (*Abelmoschus esculentus*) and Related Species," *Journal of Agricultural and Food Chemistry* 59, no. 8 (2011): 4019–24.

13. D. N. Putnam et al., "Sunflower: Alternative Field Crops Manual" University of Wisconsin Cooperative Extension and University of Minnesota Extension Services, https://hort.purdue.edu/newcrop/afcm/sunflower.html.

14. Fraklin W. Martin, "Okra, Potential Multiple-Purpose Crop for the Temperate Zones and Tropics," *Economic Botany* 36, no. 3 (1982): 340–45.

15. L. A. Jones, "Gossypol Toxicosis," *Journal of the American Veterinary Medical Association* 193, no. 4 (1988): 292–93.

16. Franklin W. Martin et al., "Protein, Oil and Gossypol Contents of a Vegetable Curd Made from Okra Seeds," *Journal of Food Science* 44, no. 5 (1979): 1517–19.

17. Robert D. Stipanovic et al., "Factors Interfering in Gossypol Analysis of Okra and Glandless Cottonseed Using Direct Aniline Extraction," *Journal of Agricultural and Food Chemistry* 32, no. 4 (1984): 809–10.

18. R. J. Hron et al., "The Potential Commercial Aspects of Gossypol," *Journal of the American Oil Chemistry Society* 64 (2007): 1315–19.

19. I. Yano et al., "The Distribution of Cyclopropane and Cyclopropene Fatty Acids in Higher Plants (Malvaceae)," *Lipids* 7, no. 1 (1972): 30–34.

20. Shiv K. Berry, "The Fatty Acid Composition and Cyclopropene Fatty Acid Content of the Maturing Okra (*Hibiscus esculentus* L.) Fruits," *Pertanika* 3, no. 2 (1980): 82–86.

21. Victor R. Preedy et al., eds., *Flour and Breads and Their Fortification in Health and Disease Prevention* (Amsterdam: Elsevier Science, 2011).

22. Preedy et al., eds., *Flour and Breads*, chapter 19.

23. A. R. Gbadegesin, T. V. Odunlade, and E T. Otunola, "Nutritive and Sensory Properties of Okra Fortified Instant Fufu," *International Food Research Journal* 25, no. 3 (2018): 1031–35.

24. Sathish Kumar Doreddula et al., "Phytochemical Analysis, Antioxidant, Antistress, and Nootropic Activities of Aqueous and Methanolic Seed Extracts of Ladies Finger (*Abelmoschus esculentus* L.)," *Scientific World Journal*, 2014.

25. Fangbo Xia, "Antioxidant and Anti-Fatigue Constituents of Okra," *Nutrients* 7, no. 10 (2015): 8846–58.

26. V. Sabitha, "Antidiabetic and Antihyperlipidemic Potential of *Abelmoschus esculentus* (L.) Moench. in Streptozotocin-Induced Diabetic Rats," *Journal of Pharmacy and Bioallied Sciences* 3, no. 3 (2011): 397–402.

27. W. Thanakosai, "First Identification of α-Glucosidase Inhibitors from Okra (*Abelmoschus esculentus*) Seeds," *Natural Product Communications* 8, no. 8 (2013): 1085–88.

28. Preedy et al., eds., *Flour and Breads*, chapter 19.

29. "Agricultural Memoranda," *American Farmer* 4 (1823).

30. N. B. Cloud, "Okra the Best Substitute for Coffee," *The Daily Journal* (Wilmington, NC), April 21, 1863.

31. John Marshall, "Save Your Okra Seeds," *Texas State Gazette*, November 9, 1861.

32. Nancy J. Turner and Adam F. Szczawinski, *Common Poisonous Plants and Mushrooms of North America* (Portland, OR: Timber Press, 1991).

33. Y. Yang et al., "Study on Anti-Fatigue Effects of Okra Extracts," *Chinese Journal of Modern Applied Pharmacy* 12 (2012): 1091–94.

34. Fangbo Xia et al., "Antioxidant and Anti-Fatigue Constituents of Okra."

35. Lianmei Hu et al., "Antioxidant Activity of Extract and Its Major Constituents from Okra Seed on Rat Hepatocytes Injured by Carbon Tetrachloride," *BioMed Research International* (2014): 341291.

36. Victor R. Preedy, Ronald Ross Watson, and Vinood B. Patel, *Nuts and Seeds in Health and Disease Prevention* (Cambridge, MA: Academic Press, 2011).

37. I. H. Burkill et al., *A Dictionary of the Economic Products of the Malay Peninsula* (London: Crown Agents for the Colonies, 1935).

38. Archer Griffeth, "Okra: A Substitute for Coffee," *Southern Banner* (Athens, GA), February 11, 1863.

39. M. M. Vilmorin-Andrieux et al., *The Vegetable Garden: Illustrations, Descriptions, and Culture of the Garden Vegetables of Cold and Temperate Climates* (New York: Dutton, 1920).

40. "Okra Seeds a Substitute for Coffee," *Ohio Cultivator*, January 1, 1845.

Chapter 9. Let's Keep Stalking About Okra

1. Credits, *The Independent Monitor*, March 2, 1869.

2. "The Okra as a Material for Papermills," *Weekly State Journal*, March 20, 1869.

3. "Paper. A New Material for Its Manufacture," *Times-Argus*, October 27, 1869.

4. "Scientific Gossip," *Richmond Dispatch*, January 21, 1870.

5. "Okra the Modern Paper Plant," *Tuscaloosa Weekly Times*, April 12, 1876.

6. *Report of the Board on Behalf of United States Executive Departments at the International Exhibition Held at Philadelphia*, vol. 2 (Ann Arbor: University of Michigan Library, 1884).

7. "Rival for Cotton Has Been Found."

8. "A Fortune Awaits the Cultivators of Okra," *Pensacola News Journal*, March 2, 1909.

9. "A Fortune Awaits the Cultivators of Okra."

10. "Every Part of Okra Plant Is of Commercial Value," *Atlanta Constitution*, June 21, 1909.

11. "Farmers Are Urged to Cultivate Okra: More Money in It than Raising Cotton, Declares John Whitson," *Atlanta Constitution*, September 4, 1915.

12. "South's New Money Crop: Okra Declared to Be Adapted for Manufacture of Paper," *Burlington (VT) Free Press*, September 9, 1915.

13. "Cotton Stalk Paper," *Wilmington (NC) Morning Star*, August 11, 1916.

14. "Dr. Miller Reports. Okra Stalks Found Good for Paper," *Daily World* (Opelousas, LA), April 23, 1964.

15. Quentin R. Skrabec Jr., *The Green Vision of Henry Ford and George Washington Carver: Two Collaborators in the Cause of Clean Industry* (Jefferson, NC: McFarland, 2013).

16. Vijay Kumar Thakur, Manju Kumari Thakur, and Michael R. Kessler, eds., *Handbook of Composites from Renewable Materials*, vol. 4, *Functionalization* (Beverly, MA: Scrivener, 2017).

17. J. D. Legare, ed., *Southern Agriculturist and Register of Rural Affairs* (Charleston, SC: A. E. Miller, 1829).

18. W. E. Sudlow, "Watch the Okra Plant," *St. Louis Post Dispatch*, January 3, 1890, 5.

19. "Future Okra Kings," *Sioux City Journal*, January 8, 1890, 5.

20. A. Rahman et al., "Fabrication, Mechanical Characterization and Interfacial Properties of Okra Fiber Reinforced Polypropylene Composites," *International Journal of Engineering Materials and Manufacture* 3, no. 1 (2018): 18–31.

21. Matthew Ogwu, "Preliminary Assessment of the Micro Anatomy of Okra," *Egyptian Academic Journal of Biological Sciences* 5, no. 1 (2014): 39–54.

Chapter 10. Grow, Okra, Grow

1. Dick Raymond, *The Gardens For All Book of Eggplant, Okra and Peppers* (South Burlington, VA: National Gardening Association, 1987).

2. John E. Weaver and William E. Bruner, *Root Development of Vegetable Crops* (New York: McGraw-Hill, 1927).

3. S. K. Gandhi and Naresh Mehta, "Diseases and Their Management," in *Okra Handbook*, ed. Dhankhar and Singh.

4. M. A. Mossler, M. Lamberts, and T. Olczyk, "Okra in the United States," in *Okra Handbook*, ed. Dhankhar and Singh.

5. Gordon Johnson, "Boron Deficiencies and Toxicities in Vegetable Crops," University of Delaware Cooperative Extension, June 19, 2015, https://extension.udel.edu/weeklycropupdate/?p=8121.

6. Gerardo Mangual-Crespo and Franklin W. Martin, "Effect of Spacing on Seed, Protein, and Oil Production of Four Okra Varieties," *Journal of Agriculture of University of Puerto Rico* 45 (1979): 450–59.

7. A. W. Salau and E. A. Makinde, "Planting Density and Variety on Okra Growth, Yield, and Yield Duration," *International Journal of Vegetable Science* 21, no. 4 (2015): 363–72.

8. "Production of Okra Using Plasticulture Technology," in *Okra Handbook*, ed. Dhankhar and Singh.

9. M. Versari and S. Guerrini, "The Use of Mater-Bi Biodegradable Mulch Film in Europe," *American Society of Plastic Surgeons* 31 (2003): 43.

10. Maddie Kilgannon, "Amazon's Jeff Bezos Spotted Having Dinner in Kendall Square," *Boston Globe*, October 28, 2018.

11. William Woys Weaver, "Heirloom Okra Plant Varieties: Organic Gardening," *Mother Earth News*, August 20, 2013, https://www.motherearthnews.com/organic-gardening/heirloom-okra-plant-varieties-zewz1308zpit.

12. L. Baxter and L. Waters Jr., "Controlled Atmosphere Effects on Physical Changes and Ethylene Evolution in Harvested Okra," *Horticultural Science* 25 (1990): 92–95.

13. Susanta K. Roy, *On-Farm Storage Technology Can Save Energy and Raise Farm Income* (Noida, India: Technology and Innovation Foundation, Amity University, 2013), ucce.ucdavis.edu/files/datastore/234-2143.pdf.

14. Edna Lewis and Scott Peacock, *The Gift of Southern Cooking: Recipes and Revelations from Two Great American Cooks* (New York: Knopf, 2003).

15. Eftal Duzyaman, "Okra in Turkey: Domestic Landraces," in *Okra Handbook*, ed. Dhankhar and Singh.

16. "Clippings from Our Exchanges," *Planters' Banner* (Attakapas County, LA), September 22, 1853.

17. *Vegetable Crop Handbook for the Southeastern United States* (Auburn, AL: Southeastern Vegetable Extension Workers Group, 2018).

18. S. W. Patil et al., "Apical Bud Pinching in Okra (*Abelmoschus esculentus*): A Review," *Seed Technology* 34, no. 1 (2012): 139–44.

19. A. F. Abang et al., "Relationship of Phenotypic Structures and Allelochemical Compounds of Okra (*Abelmoschus* spp.) to Resistance Against *Aphis gossypii* Glover," *International Journal of Pest Management* 62, no. 1 (2016): 55–63.

20. R. L. Blackman and V. F. Eastop, "Taxonomic Issues," in *Aphids as Crop Pests*, ed. H. F. van Emden and R. Harrington (Oxfordshire, U.K.: CAB International, 2007).

21. Asif Aziz, "Role of Different Physico-Chemical Characters of Okra as a Host Plant for Preference of *Earias* spp.," *Pakistan Journal of Zoology* 44, no. 2 (2012): 361–69.

22. M. A. Mossler, M. Lamberts, and T. Olczyk, "Okra in the United States," in *Okra Handbook*, ed. Dhankhar and Sing.

23. Ram Singh and G. S. Dhaliwal, "Insect Pests and Their Management," in *Okra Handbook*, ed. Dhankhar and Singh.

24. Tariq Mukhtar et al., "Evaluation of Resistance to Root-Knot Nematode (*Meloidogyne incognita*) in Okra Cultivars," *Crop Protection* 56 (2014): 25–30.

25. Harsimran K. Gill and Robert McSorley, "Cover Crops for Managing Root-Knot Nematodes," University of Florida IFAS Extension, July 2011, http://edis.ifas.ufl.edu/in892.

26. Gandhi and Mehta, "Diseases and Their Management."

27. Gandhi and Mehta, "Diseases and Their Management."

28. Tripathi et al., *Biology of Abelmoschus esculentus (Okra)*.

INDEX

Note: Page numbers in *italics* refer to figures and photographs. Page numbers followed by a "t" refer to tables.

Index

Index

Index

Index

ABOUT THE AUTHOR

Expert okra enthusiast Chris Smith writes regularly for *The Heirloom Gardener*, the *Mother Earth News* blog, and the *Farmers' Almanac* blog. His presentations on the versatility of okra have delighted audiences at food and farming festivals and fairs throughout the Southeast. He is the communications manager for Sow True Seed in Asheville, North Carolina, and executive director of The Utopian Seed Project. Smith also serves on the boards of The People's Seed and Slow Food Asheville. A native of the U.K., Smith has a master's degree in creative writing from The University of Manchester. His short stories have been published in *Nashville Review*, *Mid-American Review*, and *The Manchester Review*.

About the Foreword Author

Michael W. Twitty is the author of *The Cooking Gene*, which received two James Beard Foundation awards in 2018 (Best Food Writing / Book of the Year). Twitty is a dynamic culinary historian, historic interpreter, and food writer based in the Washington, DC, area. He is the creator of Afroculinaria.com, the first blog devoted to African American historic foodways and their legacy.

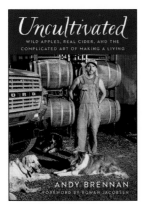

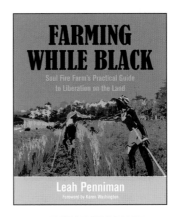

the politics and practice of sustainable living

CHELSEA GREEN PUBLISHING

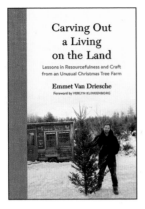

CARVING OUT A LIVING ON THE LAND
*Lessons in Resourcefulness and Craft from
an Unusual Christmas Tree Farm*
EMMET VAN DRIESCHE
9781603588263
Hardcover • $28.00

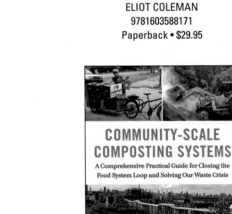

**THE NEW ORGANIC GROWER,
30TH ANNIVERSARY EDITION**
*A Master's Manual of Tools and Techniques
for the Home and Market Gardener*
ELIOT COLEMAN
9781603588171
Paperback • $29.95

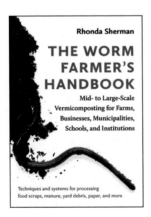

THE WORM FARMER'S HANDBOOK
*Mid- to Large-Scale Vermicomposting
for Farms, Businesses, Municipalities,
Schools, and Institutions*
RHONDA SHERMAN
9781603587792
Paperback • $29.95

COMMUNITY-SCALE COMPOSTING SYSTEMS
*A Comprehensive Practical Guide
for Closing the Food System Loop and
Solving Our Waste Crisis*
JAMES MCSWEENEY
9781603586542
Hardcover • $59.95

CHELSEA
GREEN
PUBLISHING
the politics and practice of sustainable living

For more information or to request a catalog,
visit **www.chelseagreen.com** or
call toll-free **(800) 639-4099**.